HUMAN ECOLOGY IN THE TROPICS

SOCIETY FOR THE STUDY OF HUMAN BIOLOGY

Although there are many scientific societies for the furtherance of the biological study of man as an individual, there has been no organization in Great Britain catering for those (such as physical anthropologists or human geneticists) concerned with the biology of human populations. The need for such an association was made clear at a Symposium at the Ciba Foundation in November 1957, on "The Scope of Physical Anthropology and Human Population Biology and their Place in Academic Studies". As a result the Society for the Study of Human Biology was founded on May 7th, 1958, at a meeting at the British Museum (Natural History).

The aims of the Society are to advance the study of the biology of human populations and of man as a species, in all its branches, particularly human variability, human genetics and evolution, human adaptability and ecology.

At present the Society holds two full-day meetings per year—a Symposium (usually in the autumn) on a particular theme with invited speakers, and a scientific meeting for proffered papers. The papers given at the Symposia are published and the monographs are available to members at reduced prices.

Persons are eligible for membership who work or who have worked in the field of human biology as defined in the aims of the Society. They must be proposed and seconded by members of the Society. The subscription is £5.50 per annum (this includes the Society's journal *Annals of Human Biology*) and there is no entrance fee.

Applications for membership should be made to Dr. A. J. Boyce, Hon. General Secretary, Department of Human Anatomy, University of Oxford, South Parks Road, Oxford OX1 3QX.

PUBLICATIONS OF THE SOCIETY

Symposia, Volume V, 1963: *Dental Anthropology*, edited by D. R. BROTHWELL. Pergamon Press (members £1.25).

Symposia, Volume VI, 1964: *Teaching and Research in Human Biology*, edited by G. A. HARRISON. Pergamon Press (members £1.25).

Symposia, Volume VII, 1965: *Human Body Composition, Approaches and Applications*, edited by J. BROZEK. Pergamon Press (members £3).

Symposia, Volume VIII, 1968: *The Skeletal Biology of Earlier Human Populations*, edited by D. R. BROTHWELL. Pergamon Press (members £2).

Symposia, Volume X, 1971: *Biological Aspects of Demography*, edited by W. BRASS. Taylor & Francis (members £2.50).

Symposia, Volume XI, 1973: *Human Evolution*, edited by M. H. DAY. Taylor & Francis (members £2.50).

Symposia, Volume XII, 1973: *Genetic Variation in Britain*, edited by D. F. ROBERTS and E. SUNDERLAND. Taylor & Francis (members £3.50).

Symposia, Volume XIII, 1975: *Human Variation and Natural Selection*, edited by D. F. ROBERTS. Taylor & Francis (members £2.75).

Symposia, Volume XIV, 1975: *Chromosome Variation in Human Evolution*, edited by A. J. BOYCE. Taylor & Francis (members £3.00).

Symposia, Volume XV, 1976: *The Biology of Human Fetal Growth*, edited by D. F. ROBERTS and A. M. THOMSON. Taylor & Francis (members £3.75).

Symposia, Volume XVI, 1977: *Human Ecology in the Tropics*, edited by J. P. GARLICK and R. W. J. KEAY. Taylor & Francis (members £3.00).

SYMPOSIA OF THE
SOCIETY FOR THE STUDY OF HUMAN BIOLOGY

Volume XVI

HUMAN ECOLOGY
IN THE TROPICS

Edited by
J. P. GARLICK & R. W. J. KEAY

TAYLOR & FRANCIS LTD
LONDON

HALSTED PRESS
(a division of John Wiley & Sons Inc.)
NEW YORK–TORONTO
1977

First published 1969 by Pergamon Press, Oxford
2nd Edition published 1977 by Taylor & Francis Ltd, London
and Halsted Press (a division of John Wiley & Sons Inc.), New York

© 1977 Taylor & Francis Ltd

Printed and bound in Great Britain by Taylor & Francis (Printers) Ltd,
Rankine Road, Basingstoke, Hampshire.

Taylor & Francis ISBN 0 85066 098 X

Library of Congress Cataloging in Publication Data

Main entry under title:

Human ecology in the tropics.

    "A Halsted Press Book."
    Includes bibliographies and indexes.
    1. Human ecology—Addresses, essays, lectures. 2. Tropics—Addresses
essays, lectures. I. Garlick, James Patton. II. Keay, Ronald William John.
GF895.H85   1977   301.31'0913   76-18781
ISBN 0-470-15165-X

PREFACE

The papers in the first edition of this book were presented at a symposium, organized by the British Ecological Society and the Society for the Study of Human Biology, in the rooms of the Linnean Society, London, on 2 November 1966. At that time neither 'ecology' nor 'environment' occupied the headlines as they do today. Even among biologists in 1966 the idea that man might be studied as part of an ecosystem was somewhat novel and the symposium was a significant achievement in bringing together scientists from several quite diverse fields. This was probably easier to achieve among scientists who had worked in the tropics than it would have been amongst those whose experience was limited to temperate countries.

One of the stimulating aspects of scientific work in tropical countries is the fruitful co-operation which takes place between different disciplines. The common interest in the environment brings together scientists from various fields, and the inter-relation of their work is often more clearly recognized in the tropics than in temperate regions where specialization is so much better developed.

Plant and animal ecologists in the tropics are usually acutely aware of the impact of man on the natural ecosystems. Those concerned with human and animal diseases have for long been aware of the importance of studying the natural environment, particularly in relation to insects and other vectors of disease. Those who study man, whether as physical or social anthropologists, are also aware of the important influence of the tropical environment.

Now that 'ecology' and even 'human ecology' have become so popular, it is perhaps necessary to explain what this little collection of papers, which includes several new ones, seeks to do and what it does not. The emphasis is on the interaction of man with the natural environment. Papers by Audrey Butt, Geoffrey Masefield and Rowland Moss deal with man's efforts to obtain food by growing crops and rearing animals, and the environmental constraints to which he is subject. The natural pattern of soil types determine where and how the farms are made, and the farming practices in their turn determine the nature of much of the natural, albeit modified, vegetation. The article on forests and the development of tropical countries is included as a reminder that the tropical forests which once impeded development have a vital role in economic development; the forest ecosystems interact in an extensive manner with economic factors, and in so doing have a major influence on the landscape as man's habitat.

It is important not to overlook the fact that the natural environment is the home of numerous disease organisms and their vectors, as well as man. This is particularly true in the tropics and in years gone by no one needed reminding. Today, however, some romantic ecologists point to the merits of traditional agriculture in the tropics—in contrast to the evils they see in the intensive modern agriculture of developed temperate countries—but seem to overlook the great burden of parasites to which man and his animals are subject in these conditions. Admittedly disease is part of the balance of nature and has been a potent factor in preserving tropical ecosystems. However the contributors to this book firmly believe that the ecological relationships between man and the organisms and vectors of disease are to be studied with the intention of applying scientific knowledge in practical measures to eradicate disease and to improve the human lot.

Thus William Barton has contributed a broad survey of the problems of health in the tropics and Christopher Wright and John Ford have contributed more detailed studies of the ecological relationships between man and two major tropical diseases. Angus Thomson's case study of young children in a West African village integrates nutritional and agricultural aspects in an ecological way. Douglas Ingram's paper deals with the fundamental physiological problem of life in a hot climate.

The years since 1966 have witnessed the tragedy of successive drought years in the Sahel and other semi-arid regions. The editors are therefore particularly glad to have the new contribution by David Turton. His paper underlines the importance of sociological factors and their inter-relation to ecological factors. So often ecologists have little understanding of sociology, and sociologists have little real knowledge of ecology. Turton's paper brings these aspects together in a most perceptive way and emphasises that there can be no easy solution to the problems posed by a succession of drought years, especially if in the preceding wet years the populations of man and his animals have, through the digging of wells and/or the introduction of modern medicine, built up to levels greatly in excess of the carrying capacity of the land in the dry years which will surely come, albeit in rather unpredictable cycles.

J. P. GARLICK,
February 1976. R. W. J. KEAY

CONTENTS

LAND USE AND SOCIAL ORGANIZATION OF TROPICAL FOREST PEOPLES OF THE GUIANAS

AUDREY J. BUTT

A CONSIDERABLE literature now exists on shifting cultivation and its relation to the tropical environment, but in the South American area there has been little effort to study it as part of a total economy. Moreover, the lack of intensive ethnological research there has, until recently, hindered any attempt to link the economy of tribal populations to their patterns of settlement and to their social organization in general.

My aim in this paper is to examine the interrelationships of habitat, economy, and society among three Guiana peoples. This is a study, in outline, of the different ways in which the three peoples have organized themselves for the purpose of living off their land and its resources. These differences, occurring within the same habitat and amongst people of the same technological level, help to reveal the basic factors in ecological relationships; they help us to judge which features are culturally determined, and therefore variable, and which are inescapable, given the nature of the environment, the needs of the people for survival, and their level of technology for exploiting the environment.

The Three Peoples*

1. The *Akawaio* Indians, about 2000 in number, live in the Upper Mazaruni District of the Guiana Highlands, mostly on the Guyana side but with a few settlements also in the neighbouring

* The information used in this paper is derived from my own field research in the case of the Akawaio and Waiyana and from an excellent book by the French geographer Dr. Jean Hurault, for the Boni (see Hurault, 1965a).

1

regions of Brazil and Venezuela, on the edge of the Gran Sabana.

2. The *Waiyana* Indians live on the Upper Maroni River of Surinam and French Guiana. There are about 280 in this area.*

3. The *Boni*, Bush Negroes, also live on the Upper Maroni, on the French and Surinam banks. They number about 1000.

Whereas the Akawaio and Waiyana are indigenous, Carib-speaking American Indians, the Bush Negroes have a totally different origin. They are descendants of Negro slaves who escaped from the coast plantations in the eighteenth century and made their home in the interior where they have since lived freely and independently. Hurault shows that they have kept their African heritage in matters of social organization and religious beliefs but have derived the greater part of their material culture and economy from Amerindians. They provide a unique instance whereby an African tribal population carries on much of its traditional culture in a South American environment. A study of them is therefore of considerable theoretical importance, for they show the effects which a totally different social order can have on an economy and environment shared with the aboriginal inhabitants whose own culture has been formed entirely under the influence of the South American habitat.

Similarities of Habitat and Economy

The Boni and the Waiyana have the same environment, even to the extent that some of their settlements are interspersed where tribal areas have overlapped in recent years. The region is characterized by dense, unbroken tropical forest, extending on either side of the Maroni River. The entire population lives along the banks of this river, the rest of the countryside being deserted except for the occasional Creole gold washer. The soils are poor, suitable only for a system of shifting cultivation or rotational farming with periods of

* There are also small groups of Waiyana on the Yari River in north-eastern Brazil and on the Tapanahony River, Surinam (see Butt, 1965).

fallow, utilizing the slash-and-burn technique.* Leaf-cutting ants (*Atta* sp.) are found in profusion in all cultivated areas.

The Akawaio exploit a similar type of countryside, for although they live 600–1200 m above sea level and the landscape is varied by sandstone table mountains characteristic of the Roraima Range, their area of habitation is the densely wooded river valleys or the small, white-sand savannas on the edge of the forest. Until the 1950s and the coming of direct government administration the Akawaio preferred to live away from navigable rivers at some 2–3 hours' walk inland by trail through the forest. Like the Waiyana and the Boni the presence of the forest nearby is a necessary and constant factor for the Akawaio because it provides their livelihood. Savannas are agreeable to live on because they offer freedom from encroaching vegetation, insect, and reptile life, and they afford nice views and light. Nevertheless, they are poor and barren, impossible to cultivate, have few products for gathering, and provide little to eat beyond savanna deer and small birds. They add variety but nothing essential. The Akawaio follow the same methods in shifting cultivation as the Waiyana and Boni, their soils being generally poor but with pockets of exceptional fertility.

Cultivation, fishing, hunting, and gathering are the main components of economic activity for all three peoples.† The Waiyana stress cultivation and fishing. The Boni stress cultivation, but fishing is also important to them. The Maroni River is the source of a rich supply of fish, including the much-prized *haimara*. The Akawaio, by contrast, have concentrated on cultivation and hunting. Meat is more highly valued than fish and is more important traditionally in their food supply, partly because of their inland settlements and partly because the Upper Mazaruni basin yields only very small fish, mostly 50–75 mm long and none larger than about 150 mm. Technological achievement is uniform over the entire area, any variation between the three peoples being too small to be of importance.

* Hurault maintains that the soils are too poor to produce crops more than twice consecutively. The quick invasion of weeds and secondary growth might also be included. The Boni take one crop only because they mix hill rice with their manioc plants: the Waiyana take two crops—as do the Akawaio from their gardens. Methods of cultivation followed by the Maroni River tribal populations are completely justified by the study of soils. The Boni have cultivated the same regions for 150 years, without having caused soil erosion or degeneration, using fallow and shifting systems (Hurault, 1965a.)

† Wage labour, usually for short periods, is now available for all three peoples. This is a development of the 1950s.

Although the Maroni River area is wetter than that of the Guiana Highlands, seasonal differences have only one notable effect. Akawaio are able to cut and burn new gardens twice a year. The Waiyana and Boni, on the other hand, cut and burn their fields only once a year because the level of rainfall is normally too high for a second burning.* This causes the Maroni River peoples to have a more intensive gardening effort than the Akawaio, who can spread the processes evenly over the year. None of the three peoples is subject to an exacting ecological cycle and the harvesting of crops goes on all the year round. While first plantings are made at the most favourable time, when the new rains begin, second crops can be planted at any time of the year. An unimportant exception is maize, which is always a first crop on new soil, planted when the rains begin and harvested when ripe during the following dry season.

Fishing is a constant activity, although methods may vary according to hydrological conditions. Hunting is also constant, except that a wet spell may inhibit it for a few days. Gathering continues throughout the year; the varieties of fruits change seasonally but the quantity is not much altered. The availability of raw materials is not affected by seasonal changes.

Settlement Pattern

With all the essentials in common and variations in the food supplies and activities of these three groups of small significance, it is all the more surprising to find that their settlement patterns show distinct differences.

THE AKAWAIO

Among the Akawaio the basin of a river belongs to the group of people living there. One or more villages may be settled in a particular river area. Each village is an autonomous unit but usually has friendly relationships and co-operates with its neighbours on the same river. For regular exploitation of natural resources each village

* Among the Akawaio gardens have to be burnt in the long dry season (September to December) or in the short dry season (March to April). November and April are best months for the Akawaio. On the Maroni River the burning period is November. April is normally too wet. If the vegetation is not sufficiently dry it does not burn well and the weeds spring up rapidly, so that a lot of extra work in clearing and reburning is then necessary.

keeps to its own part of the river area, there being considerable distances between each. People travelling through may hunt and fish but they are expected to share the proceeds with the regular inhabitants if they have obtained resources in the neighbourhood of a village. Within their own river and village area (which has no defined boundaries) people cut gardens where they like: they abandon rights when gardens are finished but can claim priority if a return is one day made. As there is so much land available per head of population one never hears of a dispute. Outside the immediate circle of land on which a village stands, old garden sites are usually abandoned indefinitely.

There are two types of residence among the Akawaio: the permanent village and the garden place.

The Village

Some Akawaio villages are several generations old and have been maintained on the same site for 100 years or more. Formerly, some at least were fortified with stake surrounds. Whether situated in the heart of the forest, or on a small, remote savanna on the forest edge, the Akawaio permanent village has the following characteristics:

1. It always has good gardening land nearby in the forest. (Well-drained slopes with light gravel soil are favoured.)
2. It has a freshwater stream for drinking, washing, and bathing. (This may sometimes dry up in the long dry season, causing people to move out of the village temporarily if they have not already done so.)
3. Traditionally the site was a secluded, inland one, away from a navigable river for safety. (This meant a limited or non-existent fish supply unless long journeys were undertaken to the main river.)
4. The true village has a large, communally built house for dancing and feasting.
5. It has a number of houses belonging to the extended families of the area who use the village as a base for periods of social and ceremonial activity on special occasions. The families usually come into the village for these feasts by agreement with and at the call of an acknowledged leader. The family heads are referred to as the leader's helpers (*boidoludong*).

An old village does not have many resources for hunting and

gathering in the vicinity; these will long ago have been used up or scared away. The forest round an old village is scarred by great stretches of secondary growth in all stages. Some of these may be recut from time to time but there is no set period of fallow or rotation.

The Garden Place

It is not the site of the garden place, which is the same type as that of a village, but its spatial and structural relationship to the village which is important. Situated at some distance from the village, the range varies from half an hour to a day's travel away. The Akawaio garden place has the following characteristics:

1. It is used as a family base for the additional exploitation of resources for living. Good garden soil and opportunities for hunting, fishing, and collecting are sought when establishing such a settlement. Sometimes garden places are situated equidistant between two villages in cases when the owners have interest in both villages. Nowadays, people may site them near some centre of wage labour or at a mission so that the family can maintain itself with ease when visiting.

2. Garden places are not as permanent as a village in normal circumstances. Their duration varies considerably in that some may be abandoned after 5 or 6 years, while others may last as long as the elderly head of the extended family lives.

3. Garden places are established by a cluster of closely related households, forming an extended family unit. There are usually under fifteen inhabitants, whereas a village is generally frequented by some twenty to sixty people.* The extended family group lives in the closest co-operation in its garden place. When it moves into the village it usually occupies one house there. Some extended families prefer to spend most of their time in their garden place, visiting their village centre at times of festival only. Others, especially the leader of a village and his family, spend more time in the village and visit their garden

* It is sometimes difficult to decide whether a particular settlement ought to be classified as a large garden place or a small village. The one may sometimes turn into the other according to the fortunes of the families involved. The maintenance of a communal building is the best single criterion, for this presupposes the periodic assembly and co-operation of the families of the surrounding area under an acknowledged leader in a central settlement.

place for short periods to obtain the food supplies there. Old villages are often less frequented than the newer ones. This is because the natural resources in the neighbourhood have become limited over the long period of time so that the families have to derive most of their livelihood from their garden places.

4. Garden places have no special communal building for festivities.

5. Garden places are important to the majority of families because there people can be at home without interference from more distant kin or strangers. The village, on the other hand, is the hub of social life for everyone in the region, and people like to go there to celebrate even if squabbles do occur as a result.

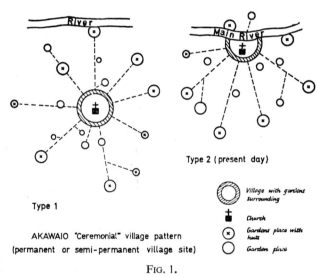

Type 2 (present day)

Type 1

AKAWAIO "Ceremonial" village pattern
(permanent or semi-permanent village site)

○ Village with gardens surrounding

✝ Church

⊗ Gardens place with huts

○ Garden place

FIG. 1.

The Akawaio settlement pattern is that of a central village with nearby gardens and with paths leading out to scattered garden places owned by extended family groups. The traditional village site was inland (Fig. 1). Only during the 1950s were many of the old village sites abandoned and a gradual move to the riversides begun under administrative and mission influence and for convenience of communication. Even so, the same settlement pattern has been maintained. Having enthusiastically adopted the English week-end the families pour into the riverside village from their private garden

B

places round. Unless they plan a prolonged village stay they arrive on Friday afternoon or Saturday morning, dance and feast for 2 days, and then scatter again.

Why was there an inland site formerly, away from a small but useful fish supply, easy river transport, and an abundant water supply? The answer is essentially a social one. The needs of defence were such that while inter-river area and inter-tribal fighting occurred it was dangerous to be found on the banks of a navigable river. Villages were often as far as 6 miles inland and the trail entrance was carefully hidden. The Waramabia villagers up the Kamarang River tell of how a party of Arekuna Indians from the Gran Sabana once found the entrance to their village trail when canoeing along the Kamarang River. They followed the trail inland, waited until dawn when they sent flaming arrows into the thatch of the houses, and clubbed the inhabitants as they were forced out. Only a few villagers escaped and no one dared to return to make another village at Waramabia until inter-tribal feuding ceased. The convenience of travel and economic considerations were subordinated to the social requirement of defence. However, this one factor, affecting the site of the village, does not explain the total settlement pattern and its persistence today when waterside villages have been founded.

Economic Factors and the Akawaio Settlement Pattern

Even small village populations of under 100 people can quickly exhaust the resources of the immediate area. Suitable garden soil is used up and covered with impenetrable secondary growth. Leaf-cutting ants establish vast nests nearby. As the gardens are cut further and further away, so the people have to travel further to their gardens and back. The harvesting of the staple food, manioc, occurs twice or even three times a week and there is no means of transport other than the human back, or by canoe if there is good soil near the riverbank. The journeying to and fro becomes arduous and time-consuming. The maintenance of a garden place means the conservation of soil resources in the area of a village and allows time for regeneration if subsequent cutting is contemplated. Garden places also allow for a comparatively easy exploitation of the most fertile areas of land within vast tracts of land round the village centre.

Any permanent settlement, however small, quickly uses up and scares away animal and fish life. Long camping expeditions into uninhabited areas occur during the dry seasons, producing large, if temporary, supplies of meat and fish. These are often devoured during prolonged village festivals. For regular supplies the journeys to and from the garden places and in the neighbourhood of the garden place help the extended family to maintain meat supplies. Gathered products—thatching leaves, resins, fruits, and nuts—are soon used up round a village or have to be carefully shared out amongst many families. The garden places open up new centres for convenient collecting.* All the products in the vicinity of the garden place belong to the extended family group there; after processing they can be transported into the village as required.

Social Factors and the Akawaio Settlement Pattern

Sentimental attachment to a certain area causes people to keep permanent village sites and even to establish garden places in particular areas. People often state that they like to live at a certain spot because their parents or grandparents were there. This territorial attachment, vague as it often is, helps to maintain a scattered population in which individual choice and sentiment play an important part.

Villages allow for a more exciting and intensive social life. The combined efforts of a number of extended families result in great quantities of food and drink for feasting themselves, entertaining guests, and receiving trading parties. No small and semi-permanent place could afford the upkeep of a communal building which is the mark of a village. Nor would it be considered necessary. In contrast, the wish to be undisturbed and free of village squabbles can only be achieved by family privacy in a garden place. Only very close kin and amicable folk join together to make such a place: a father and his sons or sons-in-law, uncle and nephew, brothers, or brothers-in-law who get on well together.

Structural factors consequent on the preferred marriage system of real or classificatory cross-cousin marriage, combined with matrilocality, also cause a family to have scattered assets. A man who cannot find a wife in the right category in his home village has to take a wife in another area and is required by custom to go and live most of the

* When hunting or travelling, Akawaio carefully note any useful resources for future exploitation—good soils, fruit trees, even a shoal of fish or the presence of an animal.

time with her people and to work indefinitely within that unit. He will make gardens for his wife there, but he may also have obligations to his mother and unmarried sisters and will want to visit his old home. In these circumstances he will often maintain gardens in both villages and have shares in one or more garden places as well. Sometimes his kin and affines will combine to form an extended family with jointly held garden places. So reluctant are some Akawaio to move away from their home area that avuncular marriage was not only recognized but consciously urged on past occasions. When a man marries his sister's daughter his sister becomes his mother-in-law and he continues to reside in the same place, in the same family, and his labour goes to the same unit as before. In this way he avoids adjusting to new surroundings and a potentially hostile in-law group.

A complex of environmental, economic, and social factors explains the Akawaio settlement pattern and accounts for the movements of the families between two different types of residence.

THE WAIYANA

Although following the same type of economic activities, except for the stress on fishing instead of hunting, we find the Waiyana with a different settlement pattern. Tribally, it is linear: that is all the Waiyana villages are situated on the banks or island shores of the Maroni River (the Yari and Tapanahony Rivers in the other Waiyana areas). They are situated overlooking the water near rapids and rocks, where fishing with bow and arrow is especially productive and swimming is safe. The Waiyana like a nice view. The gardens are situated on alluvial slopes rising up from the river. Like the Akawaio, the Waiyana carry out hunting and collecting expeditions and establish temporary camps in remote areas during the dry season. Villages have no defined boundaries but have rights over land, fish, and animals in the vicinity which are abandoned on change to another living site.

The Waiyana have only one type of settlement, the village,* which varies in population from about 15 to 70 people. It is rarely more than 10 years in one place and usually it moves every 5 or 6 years, even if the distance is less than a mile (Fig. 2).

---

* I was told that formerly a household might possess a small house in their gardens. In 1963 I saw the remains of only one of these. It had belonged to a newly married coupie who may have been seeking privacy.

WAIYANA village pattern
(regular shifting of site)

FIG. 2

Reasons for Movement among the Waiyana

1. Land for cultivation in the immediate vicinity of the village is
used up in a few years. The Waiyana like to live with their
gardens round them. Unlike the Akawaio, who are excellent
carriers of heavy loads in a far more difficult countryside, the
Waiyana have a distinct and loudly expressed aversion to
carrying loads more than a few yards along a forest trail. As
soon as they begin to make gardens at a distance from the
village, even when river transport is involved, they feel impelled
to move their village to a more convenient position. In this way
too, they avoid the depredations of the leaf-cutting ant.

2. The river near the village tends to be fished out.

3. Squabbles between families often split the village and cause
a realignment as households go off and join relatives in other
villages. The Waiyana village population is possibly more
unstable than among the Akawaio, who can cool off after
quarrelling in the village by going away and residing in their
garden places for a long period. If an Akawaio village does
break up the population is fragmented into small scattered
garden places, and several years may elapse before realignment
in a new village or absorption into neighbouring ones occurs.
Waiyana families, having no alternative accommodation,
immediately join up with relatives in other villages. They
therefore are seen to transfer themselves from village to village

with greater ease. The fact that they are not divided into potentially hostile river groups and are less suspicious and hostile towards distant fellow tribesmen is an aid. The custom of matrilocality has a similar part to play in maintaining inter-village contacts while there is no trace of avuncular marriage to counteract this.

Among the Waiyana we can see a similar combination of economic and social reasons for movement but the resulting pattern is different from that of the Akawaio.* Having no garden places the Waiyana move their villages regularly, on a semi-nomadic, linear pattern, up and down a stretch of river. They move them more frequently than it is customary for an Akawaio family to move its garden place. This is because the Waiyana population is larger, so using up resources more rapidly, and perhaps also because internal village relationships are more intense and more likely to cause fragmentation.

THE BONI BUSH NEGROES

The Boni have a totally different form of attachment to land. They are divided into matrilineages which are also matrilocal. A Boni village is composed of one localized matrilineage. If there is a split a new village is founded by the lineage fragment with its own chief and internal autonomy. The village lineage owns a particular territory around and in the neighbourhood of the village. Such lands are sacred. They are collectively owned by the lineage members in perpetuity. They can be increased by cutting new, unclaimed land in the forest, thereby incorporating it into the body of the lineage land. A member of a lineage fragment which has broken off and founded its own village and lands can always return and resume his rights. The opposite cannot occur. That is, members of the parent lineage cannot lay claim to use of lands taken over by the emigrating faction.

---

* The Frenchman, Leblond, saw the Waiyana in the Yari River area of north-eastern Brazil in 1789. They were then an inland people, living far from a big river. They had a line of villages strung out along a forest trail, about 8 miles between each. (Hurault 1965b). Presumably the villages moved their position every few years along this line, as they do today along the river banks. There is no mention of permanent villages with garden places around.

Lineage Land and Cultivation Practice among the Boni

The concept of lineage ownership of land has led to the division of Boni territories into compact blocks. Members of the village have to cultivate within these blocks or in unclaimed land until the boundaries of land belonging to the next village lineage are reached. The system is as follows: each lineage possesses a number of landings on the riverside, the land cultivated being a band 0·8 to 1·6 km wide along the banks of rivers. From the landings a number of paths radiate into the interior of the lineage land. The landing itself is usually in the centre of a territorial lineage zone. The lineage members follow the paths and make their gardens along them further inland and to either side, until they meet the boundaries of other lineages doing the same. The boundary will be the place where two gardens of different lineage origin meet. These boundaries are not so precisely drawn as in many parts of West Africa, where population is denser and there is a regular fallow system of cultivation.

So far I have described what is virtually an African system of land appropriation and ownership. In considering the use of land a South American factor steps in—the leaf-cutting ant. Owing to the depredations of these ants in established gardens it is often impossible to maintain a system of regular fallow, such as possession of blocks of lineage land normally requires. The ants cause the Boni to leave an area for longer than usual, which results in cutting down the fallow period on other portions of land. Fallows may therefore vary from 2 to 20 years or more as vast areas are taken by the ants and have to be abandoned for many years. When retaken, the former owners cannot even remember the boundaries of family plots so the areas are recut at will, the only preoccupation being to remain within the boundaries of their own lineage land.

The system we find is therefore one in which the South American environment has to be reconciled with African land use. First, lineage land is kept, but land rights inside the lineage land are flexible and undivided, so that internal divisions are often modified to meet the need for irregular shifting. Secondly, instead of blocks of land owned by households we find small portions of scattered lands, irregularly fallowed owing to ants. The resulting system is something between the outright shifting cultivation of the Amerindians and the regular fallow system of lineage lands, of some West African populated areas.

THE BONI

There are two types of residence:

1. The village: this is fixed and moved only in dire necessity. For example, villages were stable over the period 1815–95. Then, for political reasons, a move was made to sites on the French bank, where the present-day villages still are.

2. Garden places: these belong to several households jointly. They are willingly changed but remain always inside lineage land; or, by the act of cutting in unclaimed land the lineage acquires rights over the land.

The Boni pattern is of fixed residential villages, to which "ancestral customs" attach them, and temporary garden places which each cluster of households makes, according to requirements, on lineage land.

*Ecological and Social Reasons for the "Double Habitat"**

The cultivable zone is limited narrowly round each village. It is a band of 0·8 to 1·6 km, for the women consider it hard to transport manioc roots over a greater distance. They find it preferable to establish a garden place (*habitation de culture*), on an uninhabited riverside where they can go by canoe. This has led to practically continuous occupation of the river banks and of the main tributaries by Bush Negroes. In their boats they transport the harvest from gardens 20 to 30 km away without difficulty.

Villages are fixed and permanent. If a village does move for an exceptional reason it moves within lineage land. This permanence is the result of the ancestral cult. The Boni believe that the places where their ancestors have lived remain under their protection and are places where their descendants have the best chance to live happily and prosperously. The founding of a new village is preceded by religious ceremonies involving the ancestors and the gods of the soil. Cemeteries are holy places and the Boni never willingly start a new one; they prefer to transport the dead, if necessary, several days by canoe to the old one.

* See Hurault, 1965a, p. 19.

Conclusions on Maroni River Settlement Patterns and Movements

In a system of permanent villages, preferred by custom, garden places are a necessity in order to find sufficient land to cultivate conveniently and as a base from which fish and meat can be obtained further from the village. The Waiyana, living in the same area, meet the same requirements by simply having one form of residence, the village, and moving it frequently. The explanation of the differences between the two patterns lies in social factors which, providing they satisfy certain environmental demands, may therefore vary considerably.

General Conclusions

ECONOMIC

1. A comparative study of the three peoples shows the necessity of movement, either of a village or, alternatively, of garden places round a village. To obtain a satisfactory livelihood and balanced diet all the natural resources of the environment need to be exploited. These resources are not available indefinitely in one place.

2. Every part of the economy contributes reasons for movement. Even very small populations, under 100, soon use up cultivatable soil within a convenient distance of settlement, but fish and animal life become even more quickly exhausted or scared away. Products essential for technology are soon used up. The term "shifting cultivation" has tended to be a blanket term masking these other factors in a mixed economy. It has been argued that soil degeneration is a basic reason for shifting; weeds and consequent labour difficulties have been stressed and so has the ant problem and transport difficulties. (See Meggers, 1957; Carneiro, 1961.) All may be reasons for moving the garden sites, but if recourse to fresh hunting and gathering grounds is necessary then there is every advantage in having temporary gardens there to provide the staple garden produce. It costs no extra effort and is most convenient.

3. The different ways of meeting the necessity for movement for the full use of the land and its products may vary from the regular shifting of the entire village population (the Waiyana), to periodic dispersal of the people and the shifting of garden places around a permanent village which is a social and ritual centre. The Boni have

the most formalized structure because their lineage connection with certain stretches of land restricts their freedom of movement in a way unknown to the Amerindians.

SOCIAL

4. The importance of social factors has often been overlooked. The lineage connection with land and the ancestral cult of the Boni is an African heritage not shared by the Guiana Amerindians. The Boni have somehow to maintain themselves in a comparatively limited territory. It is a vaguer, sentimental attachment, combined with a pleasant, convenient, and useful locality which causes the Akawaio to maintain a particular settlement site over several generations or to return to it again at a later date.

5. The needs of security in the past determined a secluded, inland site with restricted fishing opportunities and often a dry season water shortage. These disadvantages encouraged the population to disperse in the dry seasons.

6. Structural factors, such as matrilocality, encourage movement of families between different villages and garden places where the latter exist. Individuals and families may have interests and obligations in several settlements.

7. Internal organization, the equalitarian society of independent, freely associating family units among the Amerindians, causes squabbles and disputes to lead either to the breaking up and realignment of village populations (the Waiyana) or a retreat to garden places for privacy and peace (the Akawaio). The wish to assemble for social life and festivity, to renew interfamily relationships, makes a village centre imperative for at least part of the time.

8. Death does not cause abandonment of a village or garden site necessarily. For the Boni their attachment to their cemeteries is an additional tie with a particular locality. The Waiyana may utilize an old village site as a burial ground in order to avoid unpleasant associations of death in their current village. Formerly, cremation was widely practised. Death causes the Akawaio to move temporarily. If it occurs in a garden place the family will go and stay in the village residence for 3 months. If it occurs in the village the family will go to their garden place. Alternatively, they may stay with relatives until the period of mourning is over. The death of the owner of a garden

place may cause permanent abandonment. A quick succession of deaths of notable people may encourage the abandonment of a village site for a long period, or even permanently. Among the three peoples I have selected for comparison—the Akawaio, Waiyana, and the Boni—a complex of environmental and cultural factors meets in the ecological system. The habitat, the technological level for exploitation, and the basic needs for livelihood are the same for all three. Movement is a necessity. Yet the patterns of settlement and types of movement are different, the biggest contrast being between the Waiyana Indians and the Boni Bush Negroes who live in the very same region, even to the extent of being partially interspersed. This clearly shows that the cultural heritage maintains the different response of each society to the same environmental conditions.

References

BUTT, AUDREY J. (1965) The Present State of Ethnology in Latin America: The Guianas. *Bull. Int. Comm. on Urgent Anthropological and Ethnological Research*, **7**, 69–90. Vienna.

CARNEIRO, R. L. (1961) Slash-and-burn cultivation among the Kuikuru and its implications for cultural development in the Amazon Basin, in J. WILBERT (Ed.) *The Evolution of Horticultural Systems in Native South America: Causes and Consequences*, Sociedad de Ciencias Naturales La Salle, Antropologica, suppl. publ. **2**, Editorial Sucre, Caracas.

HURAULT, J. (1965a) *La Vie Matérielle des Noirs Réfugiés Boni et des Indiens Wayana du Haut-Maroni. Agriculture, Économie et Habitat*, Office de la Recherche Scientifique et Technique Outre-Mer, Paris.

HURAULT, J. (1965b) La population des Indiens de Guyane Française, *Population Revue de l'Institut national d'études démographiques*, **20**, 603–632, Paris.

MEGGERS, BETTY J. (1957) Environment and Culture in the Amazon Basin. An appraisal of the theory of environmental determinism, in A. PALERM *et al.* (Eds.), *Studies in Human Ecology*, Social Science Monographs, **3**, Pan American Union, Washington.

FOOD RESOURCES AND PRODUCTION

G. B. MASEFIELD

FOOD resources and production in the tropics can be discussed in relation to a number of parameters. One of these is the human population that can be carried per square km. When I was Provincial Agricultural Officer for the Buganda kingdom of Uganda, I used to reckon that in an environment where soil and rainfall are more than usually favourable for tropical agriculture about 135 people per square km were the most that could comfortably be carried. Where that figure was exceeded, soil exhaustion, erosion, and dietary deficiencies began to be noticeable. Yet there are other areas of Uganda where a population of over 380 to the square km obtains the whole of its food supplies and income from the land. Similar figures are reached in some areas of south-eastern Nigeria. In Java, the largest really densely populated area in the tropics, population densities range from 350 to 540 per square km in different districts. Such figures are exceeded not only in small islands like Barbados, which has 570 people to the square km still mainly dependent upon agriculture, but in some rural areas of Bangladesh just within the tropics with densities of over 960 to the square km. It will be noticed that all the figures so far quoted are for localities in the wet tropics. In the dry tropics, except with irrigated agriculture, such high densities cannot be carried. The area around Kano in northern Nigeria, which is considered exceptionally heavily populated for the dry tropics, has only between 80 to 190 people per square km.

Another way of looking at such figures is to consider the biomass of the populations involved. Recent surveys of game animals in Africa have suggested a biomass of wild ungulates in East African savanna country of about 15 tonnes per square km. This, in terms of

19

human tropical body-weights and with allowance foɪ the proportion of children in the population, is equivalent to a human population of about 425 persons per square km—a density which is certainly not supported by agriculture in any part of the African savannas. It thus looks as if we are some way behind nature in making use of the potential food resources of this region.

We therefore have to consider how we can make the maximum use of tropical food potentials, and it is natural to start with the dietary calorie needs of the human species. The first obvious fact is that some tropical crops are very much more efficient than others as providers of calories. Sugar-cane yields by a very large margin more calories of human food per acre per year than any other crop grown in the tropics. It therefore seems obvious that, although man cannot live by sugar alone, he will have to derive more of his calories from sugar as human population densities increase. This theoretical deduction is, in fact, borne out by experience. Sugar-cane production has increased very rapidly in recent years. Sugar estates, whether private or publicly owned, have appeared in countries where they never existed before (especially in Africa) and multiplied in countries where they already existed (especially in South America). According to F.A.O. statistics, world production of sugar-cane more than doubled between 1946 and 1964, i.e. it increased at a greater rate than the human race. Much of the resulting sugar is, of course, consumed in crude non-centrifugal forms known by such names as *gur* in India, *jaggery* in East Africa, and *panela* in South America, by which an even greater number of calories can be obtained from a given tonnage of cane.

After sugar-cane, the oil-palm is the next highest yielder of calories, and gives more edible oil per acre than any other crop. The oil-palm therefore appears to have a particularly bright prospect as a main provider of edible oil, especially if and when increasing congestion of human population enforces a reduction in the world output of animal fat. After oil-palms in the calorie league table come bananas, followed by the tropical root crops, probably in the order: cassava, yams, sweet potatoes.

It will be noted that the highest-yielding crops are perennials, and this is natural because they are in the ground every day of the year to take advantage of the conditions for continuous growth which are provided by those parts of the tropics where they grow. Annuals, however much one may try to emulate this advantage by sowing them in quick succession, suffer from an inevitable interval in the use of solar energy between harvesting one crop and getting another established. This interval may, of course, be reduced as far as possible by interplanting one crop in another before harvest; this is a system much practised by Chinese horticulturists, who may take as many as six vegetable crops off the same ground in a year and achieve very high outputs by doing so, and has also been a feature of other agricultural improvement schemes such as the *lotissements agricoles* or "corridor settlements" of the forest region in Zaire. But even so, the leaf area index attained by a succession of annuals cannot be at a maximum for so much of the year as it is in many perennial crops.

Turning to annual crops; the cereals, with maize probably leading at average tropical yields, have a slight lead over the grain legumes, considered as producers of calories only, in yield of calories per acre of crop. But here one must beware of thinking in terms of a single crop rather than of the production obtainable from an acre of land in the course of the whole year. Many invidious comparisons have been made between the yields of such a crop as maize in tropical and temperate countries, forgetting that in a temperate climate the maize harvest is the sole output of that land in that year, whereas in the tropics the lower yield is achieved in a shorter time and often leaves the land free to carry another crop during the same year. However, in practice the importance of such double-cropping is less than is often supposed. Even in such a wet tropical climate as that of the Philippines, only 15% of the farmed land is double-cropped; and in India, with the largest irrigated area of any country in the world, the figure is only 13%.

It has long been observed by tropical agriculturists that the denser a tropical population becomes, the more it tends to turn to rice as its staple food crop. This tendency has, in the last 20 years, been particularly exemplified in Africa, where rice production has nearly doubled, and in South America, where it has more than doubled. The reason is not that rice necessarily yields more than other cereals, but that it is capable of a more sustained yield under continuous cultivation without the use of manures and fertilizers. There are rice fields in Asia which have probably been continuously under the crop for centuries without any conscious input of plant nutrients by the cultivators, but which can still be relied upon, provided that water is available, to produce a steady half tonne of paddy per acre. No other cereal can emulate this feat. It is nevertheless by no means certain that rice is a better means of exploiting the land for food than a good rotational programme supported by adequate use of manure and fertilizer.

We have been thinking so far in terms of calories only, but these are not the sole dietary need. The other chief requirement in human diets is for protein, or more accurately for a proper combination of amino-acids. While such a combination can theoretically be obtained from an intake of vegetable protein derived from a sufficiently wide range of sources, it is much more likely to be achieved if a fair proportion of the protein intake comes from animal sources. Considering vegetable protein first; although pulses have a higher protein content than cereals, in the tropics the yield of cereals is in most cases sufficiently higher that they provide the larger amount of protein per acre. The exception is the soya bean, which has an extremely high protein content; but this is so difficult for the tropical housewife to prepare in a palatable form for consumption that it has so far remained of negligible importance in tropical diets. The tropical subsistence farmer would be well advised to grow and consume both cereals and pulses in order to spread his amino-acid sources as widely as possible.

For animal protein, the highest productivity is, of course, obtained from fertilized fish-ponds, which are capable in the tropics of yielding up to 450 kg of fish per hectare per annum. For this class of animal, productivity per hectare is higher in parts of the tropics than anywhere in the temperate zone. In all other forms of animal husbandry, temperate countries at present have the lead in productivity, but it is not clear that this state of affairs is inevitably imposed by any biological ceiling to production in the tropics. Among domestic livestock, pigs are, in the tropics as elsewhere, the most intensive producers of food per acre of land used, and are followed in descending order by dairy animals, poultry for egg production, and grazing animals for meat. However, each of these classes of animals suffers from certain disadvantages. Pigs and poultry compete for the same foods as man—grain and root crops—and in conditions of scarcity these have to be used directly in human diets to avoid loss of calories by passing them through the animal. Grazing animals suffer in the dry tropics from an often acute lack of keep during the dry season, and in the wet tropics from an absence of grassland unless this is artificially created, which may involve considerable expense. Theoretically the most useful animal for many tropical situations would be the domestic rabbit, which can be fed on materials which would otherwise be unused, such as weeds, crop residues such as sweet-potato tops, and kitchen waste.

We have been asked in this symposium to make comparisons between the environments provided by the forest and savanna regions of the tropics. Both have their characteristic advantages and disadvantages for food production. The forest regions are capable of supporting perennial crops which, as we have seen, provide the highest yields of calories for human consumption. It is this factor, and the possibilities offered by the high rainfall of growing swamp rice and of double-cropping with annual crops, which makes these regions at present the site of the densest human population in the tropics. On the other hand, this environment has difficulties for protein production. Cereals are the main providers of vegetable protein for human consumption; but rice, the characteristic cereal of the wet tropics, is the lowest in protein content. Other cereals tend to suffer, in very wet climates, from an undue incidence of pests and diseases, and difficulties are also encountered in storing them for any long period under humid conditions. Another factor which is often overlooked is the toll taken by weed competition of crop yields in the wet tropics; to escape this it is probably necessary, though we have no accurate figures, to expend more labour on weeding in the wet tropics than in either the dry tropics or temperate zone. The forest regions are also unfavourable for animal production. Livestock in these very humid climates tend to be dwarfed; the incidence of animal diseases and parasites is very high; and there is an absence of grazing where forest is the natural cover. It is these difficulties in producing protein-rich foods which have made the wet tropics the classical locus for *kwashiorkor*, the protein-deficiency syndrome.

The savanna regions are, *par excellence*, the dry-land cereal areas of the tropics, and grain is usually the staple food. The weakness of the situation is the variability of rainfall as it gets lower, so that in the drier areas, where rainfall is at best often only marginal for cereal growing, crop failures from drought are all too common. Average yields, in consequence, taking one year with another, cannot attain

C

very high figures. These difficulties can, of course, be mitigated by irrigation, which, where practicable, gives very rewarding results in these regions; but many of them, unfortunately, lack any large perennial rivers to supply the water. The savanna regions are also the chief cattle-raising areas of the tropics, not suffering from the disabilities we have listed in the forest areas. The chief difficulty here is the shortage of grazing during the dry season. This problem would probably be best solved in theory, though it is far from easy is practice, by the conservation as silage of fodder grown in the wet season. There seems also to be an obvious gap in the animal husbandry system. The savanna regions are characteristically producers of some of the cheapest grain in the world and, where the population is not of such a density that every pound of grain is needed for human consumption, this suggests that the development of a massive poultry industry would be both natural and economic.

What conclusions can we draw from this brief survey of food resources and production in the tropics? Firstly, I think, that the highest overall productivity cannot be obtained unless there is some interchange of food products between the forest and savanna regions, rather than by each relying solely on its own resources. The forest regions have historically always served, and will continue to serve, as a source of relief food supplies to the savanna regions when drought has caused food shortage or famine in the latter. Higher populations can also be carried in the savanna regions if they import some of the perennial food-crop products which can be so intensively produced in higher rainfall areas, especially sugar and edible oils such as palm-oil. Root crops and bananas or plantains can also be produced in great quantities in wet regions, but except in a wealthy society their transport over long distances may be uneconomic because of their high water content. The forest regions will, no doubt, also supply the savanna dwellers with food products which are luxuries rather than necessities, ranging from beverage materials like tea and coffee to masticatories such as kola and areca nuts and betel leaves.

The savanna regions in their turn can supply the forest regions with cheap grain, a boon especially to urban populations for whom the cost of transport can force the price of alternative foods, such as roots and plantains, up to rather high levels. They can further alleviate the characteristic protein shortage of the forest regions by supplying meat, either as carcases, live slaughter animals, or store animals for final fattening. In theory, as we have seen, they could also be an important source of eggs and poultry meat and perhaps of milk, if production ever exceeds their own needs and transport becomes easy enough. All these exchanges between the forest and savanna regions are most likely to take place if a country includes both within its borders, so that movement of products are not impeded by the extra difficulties and costs which always arise in crossing a frontier.

Secondly, more reliance will have to be placed, as human populations become denser, on those crops and animals which have the highest productivity per acre. Such crops include especially sugar-cane, oil-palms, bananas, and, particularly where inputs of plant nutrients amount to little or nothing, swamp rice. The most productive livestock are pigs, dairy animals, and poultry. Here the chief difficulty is not an ecological but a human one: the conviction of many tropical populations that animals ought to subsist on the vegetation which nature has provided, and their consequent unwillingness to grow green fodder, grain, or root crops to feed animals. This unwillingness may gradually be reduced as mechanization makes the growing of crops less laborious.

Thirdly, the most important way of increasing food production in the tropics is by greater inputs. These may include inputs of physical materials such as irrigation water, fertilizers, and pesticides; or inputs of skill which may or may not involve the cultivator in more labour, such as crop breeding and selection, animal breeding, and better husbandry. A very important point is that, because of interactions, one input often enhances the value of another, and therefore optimal effects are generally obtained by applying as many different improvements as the cultivator is capable of. For example, if a crop is supplied with irrigation water it becomes capable of using a heavier fertilizer dressing profitably and also of sustaining the expense of more use of pesticides; the full advantage of these improvements is also not obtained unless husbandry is adapted to them, for instance by closer spacing of a crop to take full advantage of irrigation and fertilizer use. Amongst newer techniques, the importance of herbicides should not be overlooked. They have perhaps an even greater potential in tropical than in temperate agriculture, for several reasons. One of these is the seriousness of weed competition in the wet tropics, which has already been mentioned; another is that herbicides offer, perhaps more immediately than the extension of mechanical cultivation, a possibility of reducing the labour load on the small tropical farmer and so inducing him to plant more crops.

Finally, it may be asked, what are the limits to food production per unit area in the tropics? This is not, of course, a question that can be answered absolutely; it depends for one thing on what you call "food". We know that there are districts in the tropics, for example in Java, Kerala State of India, and Bangladesh, where agricultural populations exist on a half acre or less of land *per capita*. This half acre has, of course, to provide not only food but sufficient income for the irreducible cash expenses of the family, if only on taxation, salt, and a minimum of clothing. It is often forgotten how much, as well as food, farming has to provide in a subsistence economy. Almost every tropical community will have some need for timber for fuel or building purposes; the need for tree plantations has been overlooked even in some otherwise well thought-out development schemes, as in the Sudan Gezira. Many communities will also have a "felt need" for a crop from which an alcoholic liquor can be obtained by brewing or distilling. It was recently estimated that an adult African in Uganda consumes an average of 1 quart of local beer a day, and this would provide, incidentally, more than a negligible fraction of the necessary calorie intake. But considering food production alone, it is evident that the carrying capacity of land could, in extreme circumstances, be pushed far higher than one person per half-acre. On the basis of existing knowledge, and assuming that skill, capital and labour were not limiting, the most intensive form of production would probably be the growing of crops in tanks of nutrient solution. Animal food-stuffs would be provided either by caged rabbits to utilize the parts of the crop plants which were not edible by humans, or by fish-tanks. The system could be further intensified if and when the direct inclusion of leaf protein in human diets becomes acceptable. For such operations in a natural climatic environment, the highest intensity of production in the world would undoubtedly be achieved, provided that water could be made available, in desert areas of the sub-tropics or high tropical latitudes, because of their low prevalence of cloud cover.

SOILS, PLANTS AND FARMERS IN WEST AFRICA

1: *A Consideration of Some Aspects of their Relationships, with Special Reference to Contiguous Areas of Forest and Savanna in South-West Nigeria*

R. P. Moss and W. B. Morgan

Introduction

THIS paper reviews certain aspects of knowledge concerning the operation of typical plant–soil systems in relation to human activity in West Africa, and in this context presents some preliminary results of work which we have recently undertaken in south-western Nigeria.

It seems to us that to treat the animal–plant–soil complex as an environment into which man is placed too easily leads to the adoption of a static resource model, which views biological resources simply as fixed quantities to be used and exploited. These resources are better viewed as components in producing systems which may be used and developed in a wide variety of ways, and which may, indeed, be improved. We are therefore not at all concerned to reconstruct any ideal "savanna ecosystem", or "forest ecosystem" for that matter, which might exist if human influence were absent. We wish simply to try to understand the relationships which exist at present in real places. Nor do we intend to enter into the controversy concerning the ecological status of savanna, though this does not preclude the possibility that some of the ideas we present may have relevance to this problem.

The Ecological Background

Figure 1 shows the principal features of nutrient movements under forest. It illustrates the approximate amounts cycling in the various parts of the system, calculated from the considerable quantity of data

27

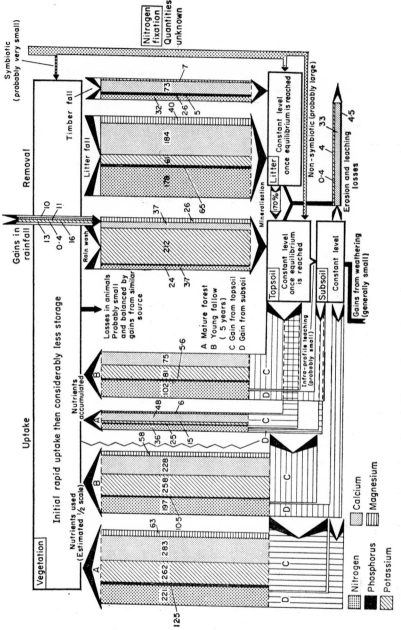

FIG. 1. The nutrient cycle under forest in West Africa.
(Note: Units in lb/acre = 1·12 kg/hectare)

collected by Nye and Greenland (1960). In view of the detailed discussion of the related problems by these and other authors (Laudelout, 1961; Vine, 1968) it is unnecessary to repeat their comments here. Such points as the fall-off in the rate of nutrient storage in fallows after the first 5 years of regrowth, the rapid turnover of nutrients in the litter, and the relative unimportance of the symbiotic fixation of nitrogen, are widely known. The generally low rate of leaching loss from the system as a whole, largely consequent upon the rate at which the principal anion, nitrate, is taken up by the plants, is perhaps less generally realized. The large amounts of water transpired by forest further restrict leaching by restricting percolation.

Figure 2 illustrates the amounts of nutrients held in various parts of the forest vegetation and the associated soils (Nye and Greenland, 1960). The important points requiring emphasis here are first that the nutrients held in the trash are readily incorporated into the soil by rapid decomposition, whereas those held in the woody parts are more gradually released, and second, that the soil store is the most important reserve of nutrients. The first point implies that burning, as a preliminary to cultivation, is an important release mechanism of all nutrients except nitrogen. The second observation indicates that nutrients held in inorganic forms in the soil are ecologically important. As a corollary to this, the significance of nutrients brought up from the lower soil layers by the plants, estimated at about 20% of the total uptake, is also emphasized (Nye and Greenland, 1960; Vine, 1968).

In Fig. 3 organic matter relationships under forest are shown. Owing to the high value of the Decomposition Constant in tropical latitudes, the organic matter cycle is very resilient, and disturbances affecting the rate of organic matter production are quickly remedied when normal litter additions are resumed. Furthermore, the humus content of the soil may remain high even if these disturbances are prolonged (Vine, 1968).

The maintenance of these cycles, and especially the ability of the fallow to restore the nutrient status of the system after cultivation, depends to a considerable extent upon two groups of factors. First, upon the ability of the vegetation to develop its extensive rooting system, and second, upon the water balance of the plant–soil complex. Inhibition of root development produces a less vigorous and less resilient plant component, and moisture deficiencies of various

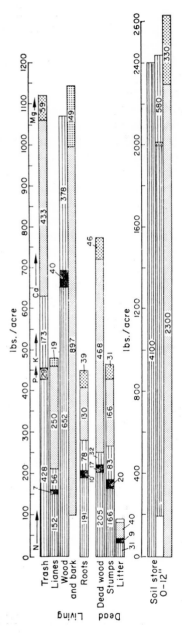

FIG. 2. Vegetation store.
(Note: lb/acre = 1.12 kg/hectare)

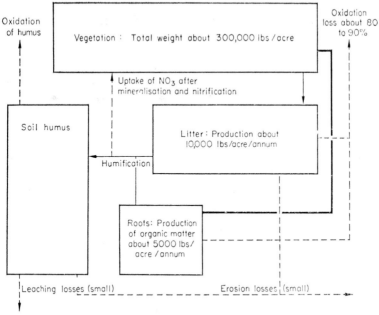

FIG. 3. Organic matter relationships under forest.
(Note: lb/acre = 1·12 kg/hectare)

kinds affect the movements of nutrients, and also the metabolic processes by which they are changed from one form to another.

Root Development

Data on the root development of forest plants are scarce, but Kerfoot (1962a) quotes a 9 m lateral spread and a 6 m vertical extent for a single specimen of *Albizia gummifera* 15 m high, and says that "the intervening soil volume is fully occupied by a network of roots associated with this and other understorey trees" (p. 24). The root systems of certain forest tree crops, such as cocoa, are also known to be extensive (McKelvie, 1962), and are often sensitive to nutrient sources in their pattern of development. Apart from their physiological functions in relation to the plants, the roots are also an important source of organic matter and nutrients for the soil, and it has been estimated that about 5600 kg of root slough, exudate, and dead roots are added to the soil each year under every hectare of mature forest (Nye and Greenland, 1960). This represents an important nutrient increment which continues into the cultivation cycle.

Most important, perhaps, is the fact that the extensiveness of the root system greatly affects its ability to withstand, and even survive, periods of water stress, since the deeper the rooting depth the less likely it becomes that the reserves of water which are tapped will fail.

Water Relationships

Attention is thus focussed on the water balance of the plant–soil system. Few data are available for West Africa, but Fig. 4 has been compiled from data obtained in the important and fundamental catchment studies of Pereira and his associates in East Africa. Apart from the fact that the forests which they have studied are at higher altitudes than most West African examples, the vegetation at

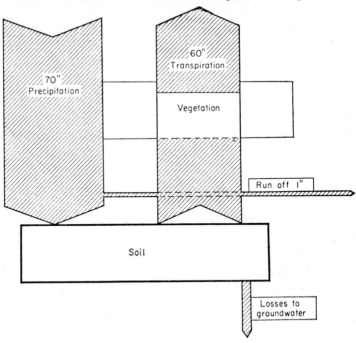

FIG. 4. Water relations of forest.
(Note: 1 in = 25·4 mm)

Kericho, in Kenya, strongly resembles well-developed West African secondary semi-deciduous forest both in structure and floristics (Kerfoot, 1962b), and that at Mbeya, in southern Tanzania, also shows important affinities (Kerfoot, 1962c).

The most significant results of this work in the context of the present discussion concern soil moisture. At Kericho sampling to a depth of 3 m regularly over a period of 3 years showed that wet soil conditions were permanently maintained below 2 m, and that, though there were substantial changes in water content at all levels above this, available water was present in all layers throughout the year (Dagg and Pratt, 1962; McCulloch, 1962a; Pereira, et al. 1962a).

Comparison of this site, where rainfall was fairly evenly distributed, with the other forested catchment at Mbeya with a 5-6 months dry season, reveals that despite the very different rainfall regime, wilting point was never reached in any soil layer in the 3 years of observation. Though some measure of lateral seepage from higher sites was suspected, the result is none the less significant. This conclusion is reinforced by the fact that two similar catchments in the same area, one cultivated and the other under regenerating bush, rapidly dried out to a depth of 1 m in June and July, and remained at wilting point, or very near it, throughout the 4 months from August to November (McCulloch, 1962b; Pereira et al., 1962b).

Comparison Between Forest and Savanna

Hitherto the discussion has concentrated on the nutrient and water relationships of forest-type vegetation in West Africa. These we now compare with those of the savanna. This term we use simply to denote vegetation in which both grasses and woody plants are significant components. We shall consider the basic differences between forest and savanna in the context of our own work in western Nigeria, which has been concentrated on the zone where forest and savanna and their associated agriculture occur in contiguous areas, and which has found its main interest in the islands of forest agriculture which are found at various distances from the main body of the forest.

The following basic differences are most relevant.

The most obvious difference is that of sheer bulk. This is reflected in the weights of oven-dry material tabulated by Nye and Greenland (1960, table 2), which, in the case of forest of reasonable maturity, is

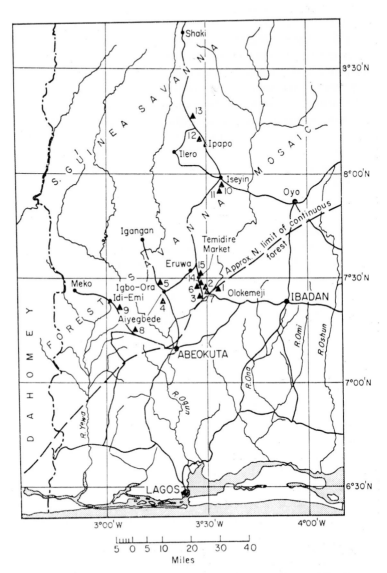

FIG. 5. Map showing location of sites studied in south-west Nigeria.

of the order of 336,000 kg/hectare, excluding roots, whereas in high-grass savanna undisturbed for more than 20 years it is less than 27,000 kg, of which more than 75 % comes from the trees. Neverthe-less, this difference becomes less marked as the volume of trees in the savanna increases. In some situations, such as that which we encountered between Iseyin and Shaki (Fig. 5), some 50–55 km away from the generalized forest-savanna boundary, the trees and shrubs exclude grasses almost completely, even though savanna species are dominant. In this case the bulk of the woody component is considerable, and may not be very different from that of secondary semi-deciduous forest (Table 1). The greater bulk of forest-type vegetation implies that more nutrients are locked up in the plants, and that much more water is transpired.

The second point is related to the first. The forest is a more effective conserver of water than savanna, and considerably reduces run-off, especially stormflow. In the East African forest at Kericho stormflow was only 1·3 % of the total precipitation under the forest, compared to 36 % in the built-up administrative area within the catchment (Pereira et al., 1962a). Furthermore, as a result of the greater transpiration, under forest the groundwater level is propor-tionately lower, but the layers above this are likely to be much moister, especially in periods of water stress. This effect is reinforced by the stable microclimate found in the forest, where the response to changing atmospheric conditions is both less marked and less sensitive than in savanna (Haddow and Corbett, 1961; Hopkins, 1965a).

Thus vegetation with a closed canopy is much more strongly buffered against changes in atmospheric conditions, especially pre-cipitation. The more marked seasonality of the savanna may have important effects, especially on nutrient cycles, as a result of water deficiency at the beginning and end of the rains (Hannon, 1949), and these effects may be accentuated by the presence of soils which respond rapidly to changing moisture additions.

It is important to emphasize the role of trees in the savanna in respect of both nutrient storage (Nye and Greenland, 1960) and water balance, for it implies that the proportion of grass and herbs to trees is a variable which is basic to any assessment of these relationships. Indeed, it may be argued that dense savanna woodland, of the type described in Table 1, is not very different in these respects

TABLE 1. DENSE TRANSITION WOODLAND, NEAR IPAPO, OYO PROVINCE
List compiled from two stands. Though floristically related to Transition
Woodland, the structure of the vegetation strongly resembles forest, with
a closed canopy, climbers, and a poorly developed herb layer.

TREES	Dense canopy at about 9 m, with some species, notably *Acacia polyacantha, Pericopsis laxiflora, Anogeissus leiocarpus, Daniellia oliveri, Lannea acida, Lonchocarpus laxiflorus, Parkia clappertoniana, Phyllanthus discoideus, Terminalia glaucescens*, and *Vitex doniana* occasionally emergent above this
TREES and SHRUBS	*Acacia polyacantha* *Pericopsis laxiflora* *Albizia glaberrima* *Albizia zygia* *Annona senegalensis* *Anogeissus leiocarpus* *Bridelia ferruginea* *Butryospermum paradoxum* *Crossopteryx febrifuga* *Daniellia oliveri* *Dicrostachys cinerea* *Ficus capensis* *Gardenia ternifolia* *Hymenocardia acida* *Lannea acida* *Lonchocarpus laxiflorus* *Nauclea latifolia* *Parkia clappertoniana* *Pericopsis laxiflora* *Phyllanthus discoideus* *Pseudarthria confertiflora* *Securidaca longipedunculata* *Securinega virosa* *Terminalia glaucescens* *Vernonia colorata* *Vernonia tenoreana* *Vitex doniana*
CLIMBERS and HERBS, etc.	*Ampelocissus leonesis* *Aspilia africana* *Borreria scabra* *Cassia mimosoides* *Cissus petiolata* *Desmodium velutinum* *Clematis hirsuta* *Mucuna pruriens* *Sida corymbosa* *Sporobolus pyramidalis* *Stylosanthes mucronata* *Lantana rhodesiensis* *Phyllanthus muellerianus.*

from secondary moist semi-deciduous forest. This point is especially significant in view of the fact that, though amounts of other nutrients are broadly comparable, the quantity of calcium in savanna grasses is much lower than in forest trees. This may have important implications for the nutrient balance of the soils, especially in relation to phosphorus (Laudelout et al., 1954; Nye, 1958 a, b; Nye and Hutton, 1957).

What has been said so far applies largely to the moderate rainfall areas of West Africa. The situations in the wetter, less seasonal areas, and in the drier, more variable regions are different in many important details (Vine, 1954 and 1968; Nye and Greenland, 1960), but it has been convincingly argued that these areas of moderate rainfall— about 1–2 m—are potentially richer agriculturally than either the drier or the wetter zones. Certainly they generally carry a higher density of population. There is therefore some justification for devoting the remainder of this paper to them.

Man's Effect on the Plant–Soil Complex

The problem of considering man in relation to the plant–soil systems revolves around two questions. First, what effects do his agricultural activities have upon these systems? And second, how do these systems affect the ways in which he grows his crops?

At the outset it must be emphasized that agriculture is essentially an economic activity. It does have clear and definite ecological implications, but the systems of production are largely the result of social and economic influences. Thus such features as crop rotations can best be understood by examining them first in relation to labour requirements, markets, and other economic factors, and then in terms of their relationships to nutrients, water, and other ecological influences.

It has been generally assumed that there is a close relationship between the generalized ecological zones and both the character and the effect of agriculture in the tropics. At a certain level of generalization this may be true. Social and economic factors, however, produce considerable diversity in the actual use of broadly comparable biological resources in any particular location, and local factors, especially related to soil, may produce striking differences in the agricultural pattern. Thus the study of particular local situations from both the socio-economic and the ecological viewpoints must be basic to understanding. Locations in which forest and savanna are found in close proximity thus offer special opportunities for study, since people of the same village will frequently farm land in both forest and savanna.

In our recent study we visited 15 sites in the area of western Nigeria between Olokemeji, Shaki, and Meko (Fig. 5). In 13 of these, forest and savanna occurred together in close proximity; in the remaining two sites similar topographic changes were present but forest occurred only as a gallery feature along watercourses. We examined in detail the composition and structure of the vegetation in relation to certain soil properties across the forest–savanna boundary, irrespective of the degree or character of the human influence in any particular location. Some 13 km of transect were set out, and along them the changes in the trees and climbers, in the cultivated plants and weeds, and in the general character of the vegetation, whether planted or self-sown, were noted. At certain points along each transect soil samples were taken and described at fixed depths. At these points also a complete list was made of the herbs present within a circle of 3 feet radius, and of the woody plants, including climbers, within one of 30 feet radius. The number of individuals of the most common tree species was recorded, and the relative cover of the various herbs was also estimated. Some 131 samples were treated in this way. Full analysis of this large block of data using multivariate techniques has not yet been commenced, but preliminary examination has revealed certain important facts which seem to us to be significant, especially in view of the manifest pre-eminence of root development and water balance in the critical internal relationships of the forest and savanna plant–soil systems.

The programme of observations described above was part of a wider project which has involved the systematic examination of the available aerial photographic cover of the area between Ibadan and the Dahomey border (Fig. 5). This cover is for two dates, namely the panchromatic photography of 1953–4, and the infra-red of 1962–3. This latter cover has been progressively extended since this date. Comparison between photographs of each date, and also between photographs on overlapping strips which were flown on dates anything from 2 weeks to 4 months apart, made it possible to study movements of the boundary over the intervening period, to obtain a picture of the changing aspect of the savanna during the dry season, and to trace the pattern of burning in its variation both in space and time. The first significant observation is that on the 13 sites which included both forest and savanna types of plant association there was a corresponding change in soil properties affecting the ability to retain moisture in the dry season in the absence of additions of atmospheric precipitation, or the ability of the plants, particularly the trees, to develop extensive root systems. Sometimes both types of change occurred together. Thus on one transect which was cut through an island of forest on the summit of an interfluve, at the northern end the change from dense woody regrowth to savanna regrowth was accompanied by a change in the silt-plus-clay content of the top inch, from well over 35% to less than 10% (Table 2).

TABLE 2. THICKET AND SECONDARY FOREST, AND SAVANNA REGROWTH,
NEAR AIYEGBEDE, ABEOKUTA PROVINCE
Lists compiled from six samples in thicket and secondary forest, and two
samples in savanna regrowth

	Thicket and secondary forest over heavy soil with mottled clay at depth	Savanna regrowth over sandy soil with hardening pan layer at 50–60 cm
TREES and SHRUBS		
9–18 m	*Elaeis guineensis*	
3–9 m	*Acacia polyacantha*	
	Albizia zygia	
	Blighia sapida	
	Carica papaya	
	Celtis zenkeri	
	Cola nitida	
	Erythrina senegalensis	
	Holarrhena floribunda	
	Morinda lucida	
	Rauvolfia vomitoria	
Less than 3 m		
	Acacia polyacantha	*Acacia polyacantha*
	Antiaris africana	*Annona senegalensis*
	Carcia papaya	*Daniellia oliveri*
	Ceiba pentandra	*Elaeis guineensis*
	Cola millenii	*Ficus capensis*
	Dichapetalum guineense	*Hymenocardia acida*
	Diospyros mespiliformis	*Lonchocarpus cyanescens*
	Diospyros monbuttensis	*Parinari curatellifolia*
	Dombeya buettneri	*Stereospermum kunthianum*
	Ficus exasperata	
	Holarrhena floribunda	
	Lecaniodiscus cupanioides	
	Malacantha alnifolia	
	Monodora tenuifolia	
	Morinda lucida	

D

TABLE 2 (*contd.*)

	Thicket and secondary forest over heavy soil with mottled clay at depth	Savanna regrowth over sand-soil with hardening pan layer at 50–60 cm
TREES and SHRUBS Less than 3 m	*Parkia clappertoniana* *Ricinodendron heudelotii* *Theobroma cacao* *Trema guineensis* *Vernonia* sp.	
	Anchomanes sp. *Deinbollia* sp. *Ehretia cymosa* *Eupatorium odoratum* *Manihot esculenta* *Melanthera scandens* *Musa* sp. *Securinega virosa* *Solanum erianthum* *Tephrosia bracteolata* *Triumfetta cordifolia*	*Nauclea latifolia* *Tephrosia flexuosa* *Vernonia tenoreana* *Waltheria indica*
CLIMBERS, etc.	*Acacia* spp. *Cardiospermum grandiflorum* *Combretum zenkeri* *Dioclea* sp. *Dioscorea dumetorum* *Dioscorea preussii* *Elaeodendron afzelii* *Gongronema latifolium* *Hewittia sublobata* *Motandra guineensis* *Mucuna pruriens* *Paullinia pinnata* *Secamone afzelii* *Tragia benthamii* *Triclisia subcordata*	
HERBS, etc.	*Asystasia insularis* *Asystasia* sp. *Cissampelos owariensis* *Euphorbia heterophylla* *Neostachyanthus occidentalis* *Phaulopsis ciliata* *Psychotria* sp. *Sebastiana chamaelea*	*Aspilia africana* *Ananas comosa* *Andropogon gayanus* *Biophytum petersianum* *Byrsocarpus coccineus* *Cassia mimosoides* *Commelina benghalensis* *Fimbristylis exilis* *Imperata cylindrica* *Indigofera hirsuta* *Pennisetum polystachyon* *Tridax procumbens*

Furthermore, the layer of mottled clay in the lower part of the soil profile became considerably harder, and occurred nearer the surface, in the savanna regrowth. These changes took place in a horizontal distance of only 5-6 m. At the southern end of same transect a comparable situation occurred. A plantation of healthy cocoa about 10 years old was bounded on its savanna-ward side by a dense mat of *Euphorbia heterophylla* 2 m wide, which gave place to a large area of cultivation dominated by guinea corn (*Sorghum vulgare*) and cassava (*Manihot esculenta*). This change, and the contrast in weeds and adventitious plants, shown in Table 3, was also associated with a change in soil properties.

TABLE 3. COCOA PLANTATION AND SAVANNA CULTIVATION, NEAR
AIYEGBEDE, ABEOKUTA PROVINCE

Lists compiled from one sample and transect data in the cocoa plantation,
and from four lists and transect data for the savanna cultivation

	Cocoa plantation over heavy soil with mottled clay at depth	Savanna cultivation over sandy soil with pan at 40–60 cm
TREES and SHRUBS 3–9 m		
planted	*Theobroma cacao*	
self-sown	*Antiaris africana*	*Acacia polyacantha*
	Spondias mombin	
Less than 3 m		
planted	*Theobroma cacao*	*Anacardium occidentale*
	Citrus aurantium	
self-sown		
	Deinbollia sp.	*Albizia zygia*
	Jatropha gossypium	*Bridelia ferruginea*
	Securinega virosa	*Ficus capensis*
		Ficus exasperata
		Gardenia ternifolia
		Stereospermum kunthianum
		Eriosema psoraleoides
		Securinega virosa
		Waltheria indica
HERBS, CLIMBERS etc.		
planted	*Xanthosoma sagittifolium*	*Ananas comosa*
		Dioscorea spp.
		Manihot esculenta
		Sorghum bicolor
		Zea mays

TABLE 3 (*contd.*)

	Cocoa plantation over heavy soil with mottled clay at depth	Savanna cultivation over sandy soil with pan at 40–60 cm
HERBS, CLIMBERS etc. self-sown	*Ageratum conyzoides* *Asystasia insularis* *Boerhavia diffusa* *Brachiaria deflexa* *Commelina benghalensis* *Digitaria ciliaris* *Euphorbia heterophylla* *Euphorbia hirta* *Tridax procumbens* *Vernonia cinerea*	*Ageratum conyzoides* *Albuca* sp. *Anchomanes* sp. *Andropogon gayanus* *Aspilia africana* *Bidens pilosa* *Biophytum petersianum* *Borreria scabra* *Celosia trigyna* *Commelina benghalensis*
HERBS, etc.		*Corchorus aestuans* *Corchorus olitorius* *Crepis* sp. *Cyperus aristatus* *Digitaria ciliaris* *Eragrostis ciliaris* *Euphorbia heterophylla* *Euphorbia hirta* *Fleurya aestuans* *Imperata cylindrica* *Indigofera hirsuta* *Mariscus alternifolius* *Mucuna pruriens* *Oldenlandia corymbosa* *Pandiaka involucrata* *Phyllanthus amarus* *Physalis micrantha* *Pouzolzia guineensis* *Stylochiton lancifolius* *Synedrella nodiflora* *Talinum triangulare* *Tephrosia bracteolata* *Tridax procumbens* *Vernonia cinerea* *Waltheria indica*

In the cocoa plantation the soil was deep and heavy, with more than 35% silt-plus-clay at 15 cm; in the savanna cultivation the soil was sandy and shallow, with less than 15% silt-plus-clay in the layers above the hardpan which occurred at 40–60 cm.

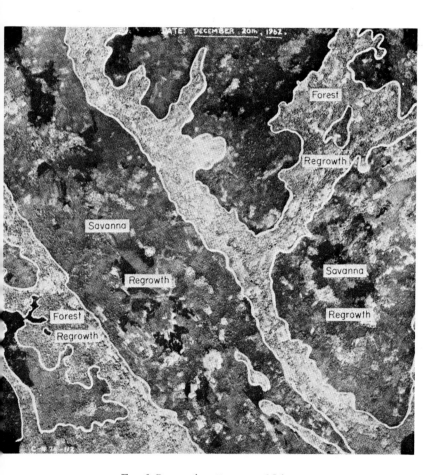

FIG. 6. Regrowth pattern near Meko.

These contrasts were closely paralleled elsewhere. In some areas, where the soil change is especially striking and rapid, and strongly related to relief, the sudden change from woody fallow and secondary forest to savanna grassland produces a characteristic pattern corresponding closely to slope features (Fig. 6). Such vegetation changes are represented by species lists of the kind given in Table 4.

TABLE 4. SPECIES LISTS FOR ADJACENT AREAS OF FOREST AND OPEN SAVANNA BETWEEN ONIGBONGBO AND IDI-EMI, ABEOKUTA PROVINCE

List compounded from four sample points in the savanna, and two in the forest. The forest, with a completely closed canopy, and few herbs, is floristically similar to Transition Woodland. It is nevertheless physiognomically similar to secondary forest

	Forest site on deep, moist colluvial soil	Savanna site on shallow sandy soil over hardpan at 10–60 cm
TREES and SHRUBS 9–18 m	Afzelia africana Albizia zygia Anogeissus leiocarpus Ceiba pentandra Celtis brownii Fagara leprieuri Markhamia tomentosa	
3–9 m		Combretum molle Cussonia barteri Lophira lanceolata Pericopsis laxiflora
Less than 3 m	Albizia zygia Anogeissus leiocarpus Antidesma laciniatum Blighia sapida Ceiba pentandra Dichapetalum guineense Erythroxylum emarginatum Fagara leprieuri Fagara zanthoxyloides Holarrhena floribunda Malacantha alnifolia Markhamia tomentosa Phyllanthus discoideus Rauvolfia vomitoria Sterculia tragacantha	Annona senegalensis Cussonia barteri Daniellia oliveri Gardenia ternifolia Lannea acida Lophira lanceolata Oncoba spinosa Parinari curatellifolia Pericopsis laxiflora Syzigium guineense Terminalia laxiflora
	Anchomanes sp. Hoslundia opposita Jatropha gossypiifolia	Aframomum latifolium Cochlospermum sp. Hoslundia opposita

TABLE 4 (*contd.*)

	Forest site on deep, moist colluvial soil	Savanna site on shallow sandy-soil over hardpan at 10–60 cm
TREES and SHRUBS Less than 3 m	*Olax gambecola* *Rytigynia nigerica* *Sida corymbosa* *Synedrella nodiflora* *Triumfetta cordifolia*	*Nauclea latifolia* *Olax gambecola* *Rytigynia nigerica*
CLIMBERS, etc.	*Cissus petiolata* *Dioscorea petiolata* *Mariscus* sp. *Uvaria chamae*	*Cyanotis longifolia* *Cyperus tenuiculmis var schweinfurthianus* *Vigna ambacensis*
HERBS, etc.	*Psychotria vogeliana* *Sida corymbosa*	*Aeschynomene lateritia* *Alysicarpus* sp. *Aspilia helianthoides* *Borreria scabra* *Calopogonium* sp. *Cassia mimosoides* *Hibiscus asper* *Indigofera* sp. (*spicata?*) *Loudetia simplex* *Pandiaka involucrata* *Polygala baikiei* *Schizachyrium brevifolium* *Tephrosia barbigera* *Vigna multinervis*

In areas away from the generalized boundary between forest and savanna the association of islands of forest with clayey soils is equally clear. An example of such a situation, described to the south of Shaki, is given in Table 5, and a similar island is reported from Ilero in Oyo Province (Agricultural Research Division, 1966). The existence of forest outliers well away from the main body of the forest is, of course, well known, and some have received quite detailed study (Jones, 1963). Though soil factors have not always seemed to be important in this distribution, in some situations reported by Jones there is real evidence of their particular significance.

TABLE 5. FOREST ISLAND BETWEEN IPAPO AND SHAKI, OYO PROVINCE
List represents one sample only, plus information from general observation in the island. There were several large clumps of bamboo within the island which were being exploited by the local farmers.

The island was situated on an area of heavy sandy clay on a relatively flat summit.

TREES and SHRUBS	
9–18 m	*Albizia zygia*
	Elaeis guineensis
	Terminalia glaucescens
	Anogeissus leiocarpus
3–9 m	*Albizia zygia*
	Anogeissus leiocarpus
	Elaeis guineensis
	Mangifera indica
Less than 3 m	*Albizia zygia*
	Blighia sapida
	Bridelia ferruginea
	Cussonia barteri
	Ficus capensis
	Fiscus sp.
	Mangifera indica
	Lonchocarpus laxiflorus
	Pterocarpus erinaceus
	Vitex doniana
	Desmodium velutinum
	Triumfetta cordifolia
	Euadenia sp.
CLIMBERS, etc.	
	Cissus debilis
	Dioscorea preussi
	Mussaenda elegans
HERBS, etc.	
	Commelina sp.
	Desmodium adscandens
	Phaulopsis falcisepala
	Oplismenus burmannii
	Solenostemon sp.
	Stylochiton lancifolium

The examples which we have quoted show clearly the floristic distinctiveness of the plant groups with which we were concerned. More important, however, is the association of the forest types with the soils of better moisture status, and of the savanna types with the poorer. This reinforces the inherent moisture characteristics of each distinct type of vegetation. Thus, even in this area of relatively uniform macroclimate, the savanna plant–soil system emphasizes seasonality, whereas the forest plant–soil system minimizes it. Each is thus a quite distinct system in respect of moisture relationships, microclimate, and nutrient characteristics, even when they are contiguous. It is thus not surprising that each seems stable under present conditions of cultivation and climate.

The stability of the boundary between forest and savanna over the past 10 years is further attested by the evidence available from the aerial photographs. Despite the considerable increase in population density, reflected on the photographs by the proliferation and enlargement of settlements, and by the greatly increased amount of land under cultivation, we can detect only very minor movements of the boundary. Almost all these are of forest advancing into savanna on the savanna-ward edges of forest reserves. Even small islands of forest are stable.

The photographs also reveal certain important facts concerning burning. Some of these have been reported elsewhere (Morgan and Moss, 1965), but they may be usefully repeated here. First, savanna burning does not appear to be universal. Some areas are only rarely burned; others may be fired twice in the same dry season. Second, the burning is most intense over the drier and shallower soils. The area of savanna grassland referred to earlier (Table 4) is one such area of intense burning, and Jones (1963), in his studies of the *kurame* of the Nigerian Middle Belt, has noted the important influence of soil character upon the effect of burning. Third, the photographs reveal that the burn rarely penetrates the adjacent woody growth at all. Table 4 suggests why this should be so, for the herb layer under the woodland is sparse in cover, poor in species, and contains no grasses. In other situations also this is basically true. For example many villages in the savanna maintain a ring of woody vegetation— often almost pure *Daniellia oliveri*—which functions as a firebreak because of the virtual absence of grasses (Table 6).

Lastly, there is a strong tendency for the development of different fire patterns at the beginning of the dry season from those character-istic of the end. Early burning is generally uncontrolled and spreads in a tear-shaped scar over an area which is rarely more than 500 hectares in extent. Late burning is less indiscriminate and is frequently closely controlled, being deliberately limited to individual fields. On early burned patches regeneration in March and April is rapid, and burning scars can be detected on the aerial photographs only with some difficulty.

TABLE 6. WOODLAND SURROUNDING TEMIDIRE MARKET, ABEOKUTA
PROVINCE

Closed canopy of trees at about 9 m with sparse herb layer, over
sandy soil with less than 15% silt-plus-clay above 70 cm.

TREES and SHRUBS	
9–18 m	*Delonix regia*
3–9 m	*Daniellia oliveri*
	Parinari polyandra
	Syzygium guineense
Less than 3 m	*Blighia sapida*
	Daniellia oliveri
	Hymenocardia acida
	Parinari curatellifolia
	Stereospermum kunthianum
	Jatropha curcas
	Hyptis suaveolens
	Indigofera dendroides
	Tephrosia flexuosa
	Solanum verbascifolium
	Urera sp.
	Vernonia colorata
	Vernonia tenoreana
HERBS, etc.	
	Borreria scabra
	Cassia occidentalis
	Cassia rotundifolia
	Pupalia lappacea
	Sida corymbosa
	Tridax procumbens

We suggest that the evidence which we have presented has significant implications, relating first to the importance of edaphic factors
in affecting the present distribution of forest and savanna plant
groups and second to the operation of grass burning in the savannas,
especially those adjacent to forest.

Concerning edaphic factors we suggest that the extreme sharpness
of the change from forest to savanna is strongly influenced by soil
properties affecting moisture relationships and ease of root development, especially by woody species. More attention thus needs to be
paid to the whole problem of water balance and general moisture
relationships, not alone on an annual basis, but also in their seasonal,
even diurnal fluctuations. Soil moisture variation in the uppermost
layers—possibly even the top inch—may well prove critical in
relation to germination and seedling survival, for example. So often
the abrupt boundary between forest and savanna is explained purely

in terms of fire (Hopkins, 1965c), but it has been pointed out that striking changes in pattern usually imply the operation of a complex of factors rather than one or two alone (Kershaw, 1964). In this connection it is important also to note that on the sites which we examined where the boundary zone was characterized by the interposition of a belt of transition woodland dominated by *Anogeissus leiocarpus* (Table 7), edaphic changes were also present, but took place much more gradually. Finally, it must be pointed out that two sites were examined on adjacent interfluves to summits occupied by forest islands. Though these two sites were associated with similar topographic changes to the forested interfluves, edaphic changes similar to those found in relation to the islands were not observed, except on lower slopes where the savanna gives place to forest galleries.

The second question—that of the importance and operation of burning—is not unrelated to that of the effect of edaphic factors. There is undoubtedly a great deal of ecological evidence for a change from forest to savanna in some areas as a result of cultivation and burning (Clayton, 1958), and the destructiveness of the late burn has been frequently emphasized (Charter and Keay, 1960; Hopkins, 1965b). The key question is, we suggest, how far these examples are representative of the savanna as a whole, and of its complex boundary with the forest. The evidence which we have presented suggests that even burning itself may not be uniform in its character or in its operation, and the real possibility that the very variable edaphic factors may also be of major importance introduces its own complications. Certainly the extrapolation of the ecological evidence so far available to the whole of major ecological zones, without considerably more knowledge of the spatial variation of the factors operating, seems to us to be unjustified.

We wish to emphasize again that we are not here concerned with the long-term changes which may have occurred. It seems to us that the complexity of these problems is so great as almost to defy solution, since any projection back into the past must take into account changing cultural levels on the one hand, and climatic change on the other, both of which are intricate and controversial subjects in themselves. If extrapolation in time is uncertain, then extrapolation in space seems to us to be equally problematical. But comparability of situation in space is at least demonstrable with some confidence by further research.

TABLE 7. TRANSITION WOODLAND NEAR ATAKAN, ABEOKUTA PROVINCE
List compiled from two lists within the woodland, and traverse observations.

Over fairly sandy soil with soft pan at 40–60 cm

TREES and SHRUBS	
9–18 m	*Acacia polyacantha*
	Afzelia africana
	Anogeissus leiocarpus
3–9 m	*Holarrhena floribunda*
	Manilkara obovata
Less than 3 m	*Acacia polyacantha*
	Afzelia africana
	Anogeissus leiocarpus
	Bosqueia angolensis
	Butryospermum paradoxum
	Canthium vulgare
	Cola gigantea
	Daniellia oliveri
	Diospyros mespiliformis
	Ficus capensis
	Ficus sagittifolia
	Hymenocardia acida
	Lonchocarpus sercceus
	Malacantha alnifolia
	Manilkara obovata
	Pericopsis laxiflora
	Piliostigma thonningii
	Rytigynia nigerica
	Sterculia tragacantha
	Nauclea latifolia
	Psychotria vogeliana
	Tephrosia flexuosa
	Waltheria indica
CLIMBERS, etc.	
	Cnestis ferruginea
	Mucuna pruriens
	Strophanthus hispidus
HERBS, etc.	
	Anchomanes sp.
	Abrus precatorius
	Andropogon tectorum
	Aspilia africana
	Borreria scabra
	Byrsocarpus coccineus
	Commelina gerrardii
	Cassia mimosoides
	Sansevieria guineensis
	Secamone afzelii

As a corollary to this we are not primarily concerned here with the questions centred around the problem of whether the vegetation is caused by the pan or the pan caused by the vegetation; or whether the moisture characteristics of the soil are the cause or effect of the vegetation. We have been concerned to examine the distinct plant–soil groups as systems of relationships which seem to be stable under present conditions of climate, cultivation, and burning. If some understanding can be achieved concerning the reasons why this stability exists, and how it is preserved by the systems themselves at the present time, then two practical consequences follow. First, we shall understand how to ensure the preservation of the *status quo*; and second, we shall be able to predict with some degree of certainty the likely effect of changing one or more factors in the complex. These seem to us to be of some practical importance, particularly to agriculture.

Farmers in the Ecological Complex

When the considerable diversity of farming practice in forest and savanna is considered, the problems with which we have been hitherto concerned become even more complex, and it is to the other side of the problem that we now turn. We wish, therefore, to examine briefly the importance of ecological factors in influencing the agricultural systems and practice in this same area.

The tropical African farmer is limited in his choice of enterprises entirely to crop plants, although other activities, including hunting and gathering, normally play vitally important roles in his economy. Amongst most communities the most important crop plants are the local staples, grown mainly on a subsistence or local exchange basis. A few communities, however, have developed a high degree of commercialization, to the extent that many farmers sell most of their produce, depend on the market for the greater part of their food supply, and choose their enterprises largely in terms of the economic advantage they afford. Such a major group are the Yoruba of western Nigeria. In this general context our area of study is of particular interest, since farmers in the same village frequently hold land in both forest and savanna, and it is thus possible to examine the use made of these two dissimilar ecological situations by the same family.

The production of crops is achieved almost entirely without

fertilizers and manures, and depends upon the establishment of satisfactory nutrient levels by means of natural fallows. Maximum use of the advantages afforded by the fallows is made by the use of crop mixtures, successions, and rotations. On the whole such fallows are not used to build up nutrient levels to a point satisfactory for a particular crop, and some of the more valuable crops may take second or third place in a succession or rotation. In many cases the operations which constitute the cultivation system are clearly the result of a regular pattern produced by deep appreciation of the ecological and economic forces involved, but such systems are highly varied and have no simple relationship to ecological distributions, even though they may be highly influenced by them. Thus major ecological zones are frequently of less use in explaining the choices made in a particular system than certain individual soil and plant characteristics, which may themselves be of overriding local importance.

Though the choice of crops and the rotation or succession is frequently conditioned largely by economic and social factors, the actual systems of production thus created are themselves subject to the operation of ecological factors, and it is these that we shall examine in the case of the three dominant systems which are found in the area of study.

First, there is a *roots–banana–tree crops* system in which the aim is to establish a permanent cover of tree crops. Until the tree crops, such as cocoa, kola, oil palm, or rubber, provide a profitable yield and the canopy closes, food crops are interplanted, but thereafter the land is kept in continuous production for 30–50 years until the trees bear no longer. Where the system aims only at the establishment of cashew, cassia, or teak, and excludes bananas, it is widely distributed in both savanna and forest, but where, as in most cases, it includes bananas with trees such as cocoa or kola, it is confined to the forest. This restriction clearly depends on the requirements of these crops during their period of establishment. A wide variety of food crops, including several species of yam, cassava, maize (usually the early varieties), cocoyam, egusi melon, and a wide range of small crops, provide an immediate return for the very considerable labour of clearing the forest, and also provide shade for the seedlings of the permanent crops. Undoubtedly the forest areas give higher yields and support more plants to the heap, but in the absence of reliable comparative data it may be questioned whether this is thought worth the extra labour required, irrespective of the need to create holdings of permanent crops.

Crop mixtures help to reduce weed infestation, and also help to spread the labour input by successive plantings, and by making planting and weeding complementary activities. Furthermore, the differing requirements of the crops help the farmer to make maximum use of the resources made available by the clearing, even to the extent of taking advantage of the differing moisture conditions provided by the mounds or ridges. It is also important to remember that many of the adventitious plants occurring in cultivation are deliberately left since they are of use to the cultivator as vegetables, medicinally, or technologically.

Much has been made of the inhibition of nitrate formation by savanna grasses in the first year of cropping, possibly as a result of microbiological effects (Meiklejohn, 1962; Nye and Greenland, 1960; Vine, 1965). It has even been stated that, as a result of this, in the Guinea Savanna Zone, grain crops are always avoided in the initial cropping phase (Vine, 1965). In Western Nigeria, however, in both forest and savanna, grain crops occur frequently in the first year of the rotation, largely because of their function as yam supports. The possibility that yields may be low appears not to be an important consideration.

The second major agricultural system involves the cultivation of *mixed maize, roots, and small crops*. With its numerous variations it is widespread in both forest and savanna, and even if it is more productive under forest conditions, the fact that less effort is required in the savanna has important consequences. For example, in several cases cassava occupied all years of the rotation and was the sole crop for half the years. Undoubtedly this was due to the proximity of the area to Ibadan, where *gari* (cassava flour) provides a staple food. Cassava thus provides high profits for labour expended, even when yields are low, in the savanna, where clearance is easy. Yams, however, give more profit per naira, but less per man-hour. They thus tend to increase in importance relative to cassava with increasing distance from the main market.

Moisture is, however, also an important factor in this distribution, and in affecting the relative proportions of cassava to yams. In the savanna yams are most important on the moister sites, and the mixed maize–roots–small crops system is itself limited to the heavier soils, usually close to the forest islands on the hilltops, or to the moister lower slopes near to the forest galleries. The greater the distance from the generalized forest–savanna boundary the more marked the relationship becomes, so that in the more distant locations the system tends to ring the small forest islands within the savanna. The sensitive element in the system is clearly the yams.

Greater emphasis on grains produces a distinct group of *grain–roots systems*. They result from the need for grain stalks as yam supports, referred to earlier, or from soil conditions, such as hardpan, packed concretions or sandiness, which make the yams unprofitable, or from the possibility of growing rice to commercial advantage.

With the last of these we are not here concerned. The first two are, however, confined to the savanna for quite different reasons. The first results from a shortage of yam poles, and the possibility of growing guinea corn successfully in the savanna, where the lower humidities inhibit the development of the fungus diseases which attack the seeds under forest conditions, and is most important where the distance from market is most favourable for yams. In the second, because of soil conditions yams are unimportant and cassava is the dominant crop, with maize or guinea corn mixed to reduce weeding and to effect maximum use of the areas cleared. Cultivation may continue for 7 or 8 years, followed by a fallow of equal or shorter length. Yields are probably low, and in many fields hardpan occurred very near to the surface, and the layers above are subject to alternating periods of prolonged saturation and intense drying. In such areas the proportion of land left to grass is high. Nevertheless the cassava grown is important commercially since it is a surplus which finds a ready and reliable market in the towns as *gari*.

Thus the indigenous farmer is very sensitive to economic considerations in his choice of crop, but an important factor in this choice is the much greater ease with which the savanna may be cleared for cultivation. His choice of crop and its position in the rotation are not dictated by ecological considerations solely, or even primarily. Nevertheless the farmer displays considerable consciousness of the ecological implications of his activities, in that he generally uses the available biological resources with considerable sensitivity and efficiency. It is in this respect that the most significant relationships between man and his living environment are to be found in relation to agriculture.

Conclusion

Sufficient has been said to emphasize the extreme complexity of the relationships which we have examined, both with reference to the plant–soil systems in themselves, and to man's use of them. Generalization is therefore difficult and may even be dangerous. Nevertheless, two facts seem clear. First, the overriding importance of moisture relationships in the plant–soil systems; and second, the ecological perception of the indigenous cultivator in relation to the conservation of the biological resources which he seeks to use for economic ends. If these two fundamental points have been made clear, then we feel that something useful has been accomplished.

Summary

This paper considers some aspects of the relationships between soils, plants, and farmers in West Africa, mainly in areas of moderate rainfall (1 to 1·8 m) and of forest–savanna mosaic. Plant–soil relationships in forest are first examined, with reference to nutrient balance, moisture conditions, and microclimate, and then comparison is made with savanna conditions. Moisture relationships, and the critical role of soils in these, receive special consideration, as does the role of the root system, both as a source of nutrients, and as an agent of water uptake by the vegetation, especially the relationship between root spread and the ability to obtain water. It is of fundamental importance that savanna systems emphasize seasonality, whereas forest systems minimize it, even in areas of similar macroclimate.

In studying the effect of man on soil–plant systems in western Nigeria, a close association between forest-type plant groups and the heavier, deeper, more homogeneous soils was apparent. Under present conditions of climate and cultivation the local plant–soil systems appear stable in relation to one another. Evidence for this comes in part from field observation and in part from aerial photographs. The latter reveal extreme variability in dry-season burning patterns both in space and in time. Thus in seeking explanations of the phenomena investigated it was clear that more attention should be devoted to seasonal and shorter period fluctuations in moisture relationships, and to the variability of both edaphic factors and burning operations.

The part played by farmers in the soil–plant systems can only be understood by reference to a thorough knowledge of their economic

E

relationships, for whatever the soil–plant–farmer relations, the choice of crop enterprise is, in the first place, an economic question. Three crop systems are examined to show the interplay of economic and ecological factors in their operation and location. An extremely important feature in the choice between savanna and forest locations is the relative cost of clearance or reclearance, and subsequent weeding operations. Rotations exist not only to provide a sequence of nutrient demands on the soil, but also to satisfy other problems, such as the incidence of disease, or the support of yam vines.

In the complex of relationships two major factors are outstanding, namely the moisture relationships in the soil–plant systems, and the ecological perception of the indigenous cultivator in satisfying his economic ends.

References

AGRICULTURAL RESEARCH DIVISION (1966) *Annual Report of the Soil Survey Section*. 1965–66, Ministry of Agriculture and Natural Resources, Ibadan, Nigeria.

CHARTER, J. R. and KEAY, R. W. J. (1960) Assessment of the Olokemeji fire-control experiment (Investigation 254) 28 years after institution, *Nig. For. Inf. Bull.*, No. 3.

CLAYTON, W. D. (1958) Secondary vegetation and the transition to savanna near Ibadan, Nigeria, *J. Ecol.*, **46**, 217–38.

DAGG, M. and PRATT, M. A. C. (1962) The Sambret and Lagan experimental catchments; the relation of stormflow to incident rainfall, *E. Afr. Agric. and For. J.*, **27**, 31–5.

HADDOW, A. J. and CORBETT, P. S. (1961) Entomological studies from a high tower in the Mpanga Forest, Uganda. II. Observations on certain environmental factors at different levels, *Trans. Roy. Ent. Soc.* **113**, 257–69.

HANNON, N. (1949) The nitrogen economy of the Hawkesbury sandstone soils around Sydney. The role of native legumes, unpublished thesis, University of Sydney, Australia, quoted in MORRIS, D. C. (1956) Legumes and the *Rhizobium* symbiosis, *Emp. J. Expt. Agric.*, **24**, 247–70.

HOPKINS, B. (1965a) Vegetation of the Olokemeji Forest Reserve, III. The microclimates with special reference to their seasonal changes, *J. Ecol.* **53**, 125–38.

HOPKINS, B. (1965b) Observations on savanna burning in the Olokemeji Forest Reserve, *J. Appl. Ecol.*, **2**, 367–82.

HOPKINS, B. (1965c) *Forest and Savanna*, Heinemann, Ibadan and London.

JONES, E. W. (1963) The forest outliers in the Guinea zone of Northern Nigeria, *J. Ecol.*, **51**, 415–34.

KERFOOT, O. (1962a) The vegetation of the Sambret and Lagan experimental catchments, *E. Afr. Agric. and For. J.*, **27**, 23.

KERFOOT, O. (1962b) Root systems of forest trees, shade trees, and tea bushes, *E. Afr. Agric. and For. J.*, **27**, 24.

KERFOOT, O. (1962c) The vegetation of the Mbeya Peak Experimental Catchment areas, *E. Afr. Agric. and For. J.*, **27**, 110.

KERSHAW, K. A. (1964) *Quantitative and Dynamic Ecology*, Arnold, London.

LAUDELOUT, H. (1961) *Dynamics of Tropical Soils in Relation to their Fallowing Techniques*, F.A.O. Rome.

LAUDELOUT, H., GERMAN, R. and KESLEY, W. (1954) Preliminary results on the chemical dynamics of grass fallows and of pastures at Yangambi, *Trans. 5th Int. Congr. Soil Sci.*, **2**, 312–21.

MCCULLOCH, J. S. G. (1962a) The Sambret and Lagan Experimental Catchments: measurements of rainfall and evaporation, *E. Afr. Agric. and For J.*, **27**, 27–30.

MCCULLOCH, J. S. G. (1962b) Effects of peasant cultivation practices in steep streamsource valleys: measurement of rainfall and evaporation, *E. Afr. Agric. and For. J.*, **27**, 115–17.

MCKELVIE, A. D. (1962) Cocoa: physiology, chapter 18, part B, in *Agriculture and Land Use in Ghana*, edited by J. B. WILLS, Oxford University Press, London, pp. 256–9.

MEIKLEJOHN, J. (1962) Microbiology of the nitrogen cycle in some Ghana soils, *Emp. J. Expt. Agric.*, **30**, 115–26.

MORGAN, W. B. and MOSS, R. P. (1965) Savanna and forest in Western Nigeria, *Africa*, **35**, 286–94.

NYE, P. H. (1958a) The relative importance of fallows and soils in storing plant nutrients in Ghana, *J. West Afr. Sci. Assoc.*, **4**, 31–49.

NYE, P. H. (1958b) The mineral composition of some shrubs and trees in Ghana, *J. West Afr. Sci. Assoc.*, **4**, 91–8.

NYE, P. H. and GREENLAND, D. J. (1960) *The Soil under Shifting Cultivation*, Commonwealth Bur. Soils Tech. Comm., **51**.

NYE, P. H. and HUTTON, R. G. (1957) Some preliminary analyses of fallows and cover crops at the West African Institute for Oil Palm Research, Benin, *J. West Afr. Inst. for Oil Palm Res.*, **2**, 237–43.

PEREIRA, H. C., DAGG, M. and HOSEGOOD, P. H. (1962a) The Sambret and Lagan Experimental Catchments: the water balance of both treated and control valleys, *E. Afr. Agric. and For. J.*, **27**, 36–41.

PEREIRA, H. C., DAGG, M. and HOSEGOOD, P. H. (1962b) Effects of peasant cultivation practices in steep valleys: the water balance of the cultivated and control catchments, *E. Afr. Agric. and For. J.*, **27**, 118–22.

VINE, H. (1954) Is the lack of fertility of tropical African soils exaggerated? *Proc. 2nd Inter.-Afr. Soils Conf.*, **1**, 389–412.

VINE, H. (1968) Developments in the study of soils and shifting agriculture in tropical Africa, *The Soil Resources of Tropical Africa* (ed. Moss, R. P.), ch. 5, pp. 89–119. Cambridge.

SOILS, PLANTS AND FARMERS IN WEST AFRICA

Part 2: Further Examination of the Role of Edaphic Factors and Cropping Patterns in South-West Nigeria

R. P. Moss

Introduction

IN the previous article Moss and Morgan argued that the present pattern of forest/woody-fallow and savanna/grassy-fallow in the forest-savanna zone of Western Nigeria was stable, despite increasing cultivation pressure brought about by a growing rural population and the demands of the expanding populations of the large towns in the urban crescent of Yorubaland. The stability was attributed to the interaction of edaphic factors, which reinforce the ecological characteristics of the forest and savanna plant-soil systems, with deliberate control of cultivation practices especially burning, in the context of essentially conservative agricultural systems developed by the indigenous cultivators. The edaphic factors of principal concern were those affecting soil water retention and disposal, the holding and supply of nutrient elements, and the ease with which the plants, especially forest species, can develop their root systems to a physiological optimum. More recent work has confirmed both the intrinsic ecological significance of these factors, and their particular importance in relation to the vegetation/land-use pattern in South-West Nigeria. This second part to the original paper reviews some of these more recent developments.

59

General Background

Recent reviews (e.g. Rodin and Bazilevich, 1967, *inter alia*) have confirmed the resilience of mineral and organic matter cycles in tropical closed forests, and the contrast with savanna, together with the significance of seasonality in savanna, and the minimal importance of it in closed forest. These features depend to a significant degree upon the water cycle in the plant-soil system and its relations to the microclimatic characteristics in the vegetation layers, the following factors being of special importance:

1. The exchange of air between the atmosphere above and below the forest canopy is very sluggish. Thus the air below the canopy responds only slowly and with a reduced amplitude of fluctuation to changes in the state of the atmosphere above it. Turbulence and general air movement are usually small, and temperature conditions more equable both diurnally and seasonally, below the canopy. Thus since the vapour pressure difference across both the plant/atmosphere and soil/atmosphere interfaces tends to remain small owing to the high relative humidity which is so maintained, transpiration and evaporation rates are slow, and water loss from both plants and soil inconsiderable.

2. Soil moisture levels beneath the forest canopy fluctuate only slowly in response to variations in the atmospheric water supply, and rarely succumb to the development even of considerable water stress outside the canopy. There turbulence and seasonal and diurnal variations in relative humidities induce the high mean levels of evapo-transpiration noted in the first part of this paper.

3. The maintenance of high rates of transpiration, and therefore of the constant level of activity in forest-type vegetation, depends not only upon the ability of the soil to hold moisture, but also upon the volume of soil that the plants are exploiting as a source of water. This will depend in part upon the ease with which the plants are able to develop their roots in the solum.

The significance of the three sets of edaphic factors to these relationships is thus clear. The perseverance of woody fallow conditions under cultivation pressure is thus likely to be considerably affected by these factors in particular locations, especially those influencing root development.

Recent work on the root systems of woody perennials has revealed a number of significant facts (Lyr and Hoffmann, 1967; Rogers and Head, 1969). Downward penetration is limited not only by rock layers and hardpans, but also by compact layers within the solum, and different species display differing capacities for such penetration. In the tropics, where compact and hard layers are common—even if rock-like ferruginous and aluminous deposits are not so extensive as was once thought—these characteristics of root development are clearly of great potential ecological importance.

Furthermore, in many woody perennials, irrespective of the disparate sizes of plant arising from genetic and taxonomic differences, the stem/root ratio (which expresses the amount of sub-aerial biomass supported by a given root system) has been shown to vary from 2 : 1 in a well-structured fertile loam, to 1 : 1 in a sand poor in nutrients. A similar pattern of variation emerges when the lateral spread of roots and subaerial parts is compared—the root spread being proportionately greater in the poorer soils. Thus in poor sandy soils woody perennials need to develop a more extensive root system in order to support the same sub-aerial biomass. Where sandiness and nutrient deficiencies are associated with layers inhibiting root development, it is therefore very likely that woody vegetation will be especially vulnerable to environmental and human pressures.

The sensitive response of root development to localized nutrient sources has also been confirmed, but has also shown that this reaction is much more complex than was once thought. Root competition is another factor which needs to be taken into account in the field situation.

It is clear therefore that the development of the root systems of tropical woody plants is likely to be considerably influenced by the homogeneity or heterogeneity of the solum with respect to both its physical and its chemical properties, and it is noteworthy that Baeyens (1949) emphasized the importance of soil profile heterogeneity as an edaphic factor in tropical agriculture a quarter of a century ago.

Thus soil properties affecting the extension and spatial pattern of root development are of great potential importance in relation to tropical woody vegetation, especially in situations likely to involve cultivation pressure. The development of the root system must affect the ability of such vegetation to withstand, perhaps even survive, periods of water stress or fire damage, or cultivation practices and short fallow periods, and the presence of compact or hard layers in the solum within the potential rooting volume of the plants is thus an important edaphic factor.

At Birmingham University a detailed study of savanna burning patterns from aerial photographs has begun, and has confirmed the conclusions reached earlier. In addition it has shown that probably no more than one third of the savanna is burned in any one year, even in the most intensely burned areas. In many areas the proportion is considerably less. Furthermore, the average area of burns *decreases* as the dry season progresses, and also decreases the more densely cultivated the area is. This indicates that there is increasing control of fire-spread the later the burn takes place, and greater control the more cultivated land there is in the area. This is especially true in the forest-savanna mosaic, and somewhat less so farther north, where forest islands are absent. These differences probably reflect cultural factors rather than physical factors, in relation to the purpose of burning, and its place in the sequence of agricultural and other activities characteristic of the particular communities involved. Thus it is very difficult to elucidate the influence of fire as an ecological factor in relation to the present (or the past) pattern of forest and savanna, without taking account of these cultural factors, and the physical constraints on fire-spread, so fully dealt with by Batchelder and Hirt (1966).

The Pattern in South-West Nigeria

The confirmation of the general ecological background set out in the first part of the paper leads naturally into a more detailed examination of the pattern in the area of principal concern. This has been achieved by analysis and investigation of the data obtained from the field observations, and these fall into two sections: first, multivariate analysis of the transect data, and second, more detailed consideration of cropping patterns in villages holding land in both forest and savanna. To these attention is now given.

Results of analysis of transect data

Analysis of the soil and vegetation data from the transects has strikingly confirmed the correspondence of the location of islands of forest and woody fallow with soils favourable to nutrient supply, moisture retention, and pre-eminently the development of the optimum root system.

The data from the sample sites located along the randomly located transects across the forest-savanna boundary were subjected to Principal Components Analysis, using programmes developed for the soils and vegetation of the Cotswold beechwoods by Barkham and Norris in Birmingham (1968). In the present context it is not relevant to discuss in detail the methods used, but it is necessary to point out that they emphasize, exemplify and quantify the general trends present in the data matrix of sites and properties. Q-mode analysis was first performed, comparing sample sites with one another in terms of properties. The total plant data, in the form of simple presence/absence criteria for those species occurring on more than 5% of the sites, yielded five components collectively accounting for about 70% of the total variance present; the first three, which were readily interpretable, accounted for nearly 60% of the variance. The total soil data were dealt with slightly differently because of the scalar measures used for the soil properties at standard depths; these measures ensured comparability with the field methods of the Western Region Chemistry and Soil Survey Division. Five components again accounted for a high proportion of the total variance, and the first two were easily interpreted and accounted for over 50% of the total variance present in the soil data. R-mode analysis—the comparison of variables or properties in terms of their occurrence on sample sites—was also performed, but the results of this are not directly relevant to the present discussion. In the Q-mode analysis print-outs of the intermediate similarity matrices involved in the computation were obtained, in order to assist in the ecological interpretation of the components extracted. At a later stage the component values for three plant and three soil components for each sample point were included to produce a new correlation matrix of the component values and plant data compared in terms of sites, and a similar one for component values and soil variables. These assisted in the interpretation of the ecological significance of the principal components.

Where individual transects included sufficient sample points (16 or more), or where shorter transects could be validly grouped on the basis of geographical proximity, a similar Q-mode analysis was performed on the smaller data matrices thus obtained. These were then used for comparison with the results obtained in respect of the total data for the transects concerned.

The results of the computations for the individual transects or groups are displayed in Figures 1 to 5. Each shows the value on the named component for each sample point along the transect, and for each point there is a value for the primary component for vegetation and for soil, based on the total data, and a second value for each derived by computation from the data for that transect alone. In these diagrams the values for the second and third components are not included.

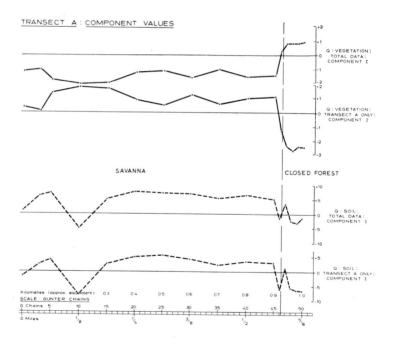

Fig. 1.

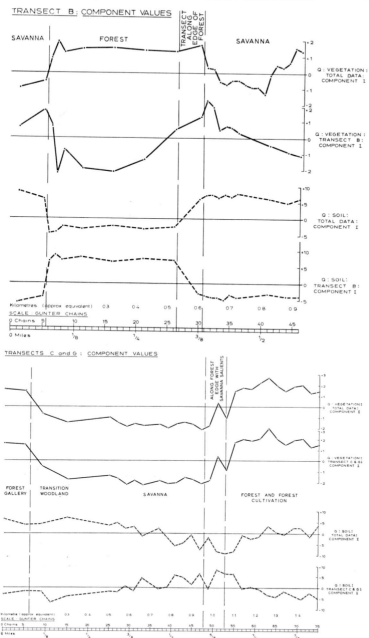

Figs. 2 and 3.

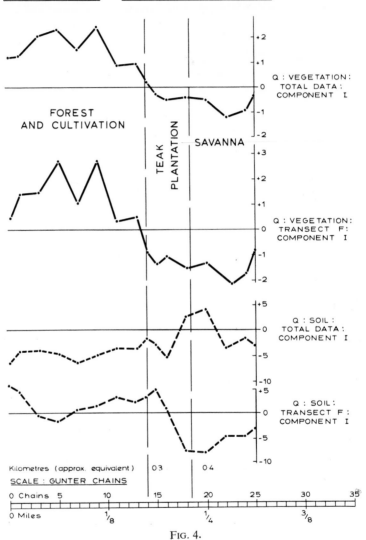

FIG. 4.

TRANSECT P : COMPONENT VALUES

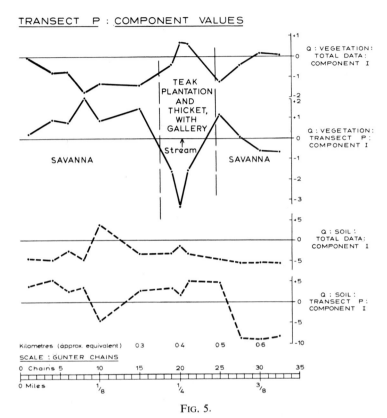

FIG. 5.

Interpretation of the vegetation components is readily achieved by comparing the association of high and low component values with particular groups of plant species. On this basis Component I defines an axis of variability between typical high and secondary forest species at one end, and characteristic savanna species at the other; and Component II defines an axis between woody species at one extreme and herbaceous and cultivated species (including perennial tree crops) at the other.

The first two soil components are also readily interpretable by the examination of the association of particular groups of properties with particular ranges of component values. Component I groups deep, friable, homogeneous soils of relatively high clay content at one end, with coarse sandy soils, low in clay, and with hard or compact layers in the solum above 60 cm at the other. Component II relates to soil colour, and defines an axis of variation from reddish or brownish soils at one end to grey soils with sepia or ochre mottling at the other, the colour change being associated with a site variation from summit and upper slope soils at one end to lower slope and bottom soils at the other.

The most striking relationships revealed by the Figures are:

1. The values on Vegetation Component I and Soil Component I, whether computed from the total data or the transect data, change rapidly at the boundary between forest/woody-fallow and savanna/grassy-fallow as it was delimited in the field, and on the aerial photographs;

2. This rapid change occurs irrespective of whether the particular transect is associated with cultivation, early fallow, or developed vegetation types;

3. The change is always in the same direction; that is the vegetation change from forest types to savanna types is always associated with a corresponding change in soil from heavier, homogeneous, friable types to light, heterogeneous, coarser types with a tendency to compaction. Here it is relevant to remark that the $+$ ve and $-$ ve directions of a particular component in a particular case is an accident of computation, and that the fact that the component trends are in some cases sympathetic and in others antithetic is of no ecological importance;

4. In the case of Transect P (Fig. 5) across an area of gallery forest the soil component values change less strikingly than the vegetation component values, and the correspondence between the changes is much less close. Here the extra factor of groundwater levels is important. In all the locations remote from watercourses the correspondence between the soil and vegetation components are much more clearly in phase;

5. Figure 6, which shows the values on Soil Component II for Transects C and G combined, there is a discernible relationship between it and the forest-savanna Component, though less striking than for Soil Component I.

Thus it is clear that the forest/woody-fallow and savanna/grassy-fallow boundary in this area is closely associated with an abrupt

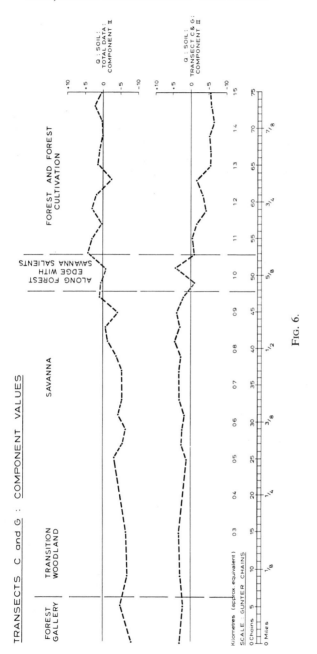

FIG. 6.

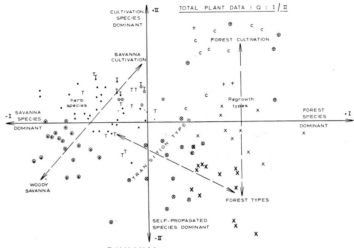

SAVANNA

WOODY SAVANNA

CULTIVATION IN SAVANNA

GRASS FALLOW

T　TEAK PLANTATION

FIG. 7.

and significant change in edaphic conditions, which is strongly related to the soil properties shown to be, on *a priori* grounds, likely to be of maximum significance to the maintenance of woody vegetation under stress conditions. In every case the forest types occur on the soils most favourably endowed in these respects.

Display of the vegetation relationships in relation to agricultural land use may be achieved in quite a different way. In the field each sample location was categorized by a simple land use class. These are listed and symbolized in the key to Figure 7. By treating two Components as simple two-dimensional orthogonal axes individual sample points may be plotted uniquely on the graph thus created. If each sample point is then denoted by its appropriate land use symbol, then distinctive groupings of points may be discerned if they exist. Figure 7 illustrates this for Vegetation Components I and II, and Figure 8 for II and III. The following groupings and gradients may be readily distinguished:

1. From woody and grassy savanna types through transition woodland to secondary and high forest types. This appears to represent the succession involved in the advance of forest into savanna in suitable sites, especially in Forest Reserves;

2. From woody savanna types through more grassy types to grass-herb fallows and savanna cultivation. This clearly implies the normal savanna succession after the abandonment of cultivation;

3. From high and secondary forest types through low secondary forest and thicket to forest cultivation, including both food and perennial tree crops. This represents the normal woody fallow succession.

In Figure 8 the two fallow successions are more clearly displayed, and are shown to be quite independent of one another. There is a notable absence of evidence in any of the displays of the data of a discernible sequence leading from forest or forest cultivation to any of the savanna types. This strongly confirms the evidence of the aerial photographs, which provide no indication of any tendency for savanna types to advance into forest areas in the area of study between 1952 and 1962. The only detectable movement is an advance of forest into savanna in certain edaphically favoured locations. Even the most complicated convolutions of the mapped boundary, and the smallest detectable patches of forest, seem to have been preserved almost intact throughout 10 years of rapidly increasing cultivation pressure.

Thus the detailed analyses of the data seem to confirm clearly the evidence of the aerial photographs and preliminary analysis of field observations and general appraisal. There are in this area two strongly contrasting plant-soil systems with strong agricultural impacts within them which exist in a stable juxtaposition at the present time, and, furthermore, this stability has been maintained despite increasing cultivation pressure resulting from a growing local population, and the demands of rapidly expanding towns in the vicinity.

This is, of course, not a comment on the possibility or characreristics of vegetation changes in the more remote past, though

F

these questions are obviously not completely unrelated. It is clearly possible to argue, for example, that in the present state of knowledge concerning tropical pedogenesis the compaction and sandiness of the savanna soils is the result rather than the cause of the present pattern of vegetation types. It is necessary to insist, however, that consequent upon the relations between edaphic factors and the complicated cultural dimensions of the practice of burning, the present agro-ecological situation is at least conditionally stable.

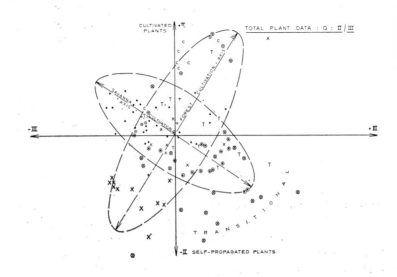

⊗   TRANSITION WOODLAND

✗   HIGH, AND HIGH SECONDARY, FOREST

✗   LOW SECONDARY FOREST AND DENSE THICKET

+   LOW BUSH REGROWTH

⊕   CULTIVATION IN FOREST

C   COCOA PLANTATIONS

FIG. 8.

The significance of cropping patterns

The cultural implications of burning and cultivation in relation to vegetation and edaphic factors lead naturally into a further consideration of the agricultural significance of forest and savanna, especially islands of forest in the savanna. This has been discussed in detail recently (Morgan and Moss, 1970), but it is necessary to emphasize some of the main points here, and to present the results of some observations on cropping patterns in villages which hold land in both forest and savanna.

Two important preliminary points need to be made. First, the Yoruba farmers in the area are highly commercial in their farming, with a high proportion of their land devoted to crops for sale, both perennial tree crops and food crops; and second, the holdings are often large, 10 hectares or more in area of cropped land, and sometimes up to 16 hectares. Such large holdings need hired labour to work them, 3 hectares being about the maximum cultivable by the average farmer without hired help. Some of this labour is local, but with increasing migration of the young to the local large towns seasonal labour is obtained from much farther afield—Igbirra and Tiv labourers being fairly common on the larger holdings. Thus in the area we are not dealing with a simple situation of dominantly subsistence cropping with particular cash crops as a supplement, but with an integrated commercial system which is geared as a whole to local and national demand, and which is developing in response to changing economic and social pressures. In this response the farmer seems to be fully cognisant of the potential and hazards of the ecological conditions from which he is producing his crops.

Figure 9 illustrates the pattern of cropping in 302 fields examined on holdings including land in both forest and savanna. It has been compiled from data already published (Morgan and Moss, 1970) and is designed to emphasize the complexity of cropping patterns in the situation under scrutiny. The fields sampled relate to holdings associated with particular villages, and in no sense constitute a fully systematic, let alone random, sample of fields. Nevertheless certain very significant points emerge. First of all, there is a number of crops found both in forest and savanna, as well as on the fringe land between (see below), cassava, maize and yams being especially important. But investigation revealed that cassava grown sole in savanna was entirely for sale as *gari* prepared by the women of the village. Second, some crops with specific ecological requirements, such as cocoa, bananas and cocoyam were confined to the forest or forest edge, whereas guinea corn was confined to the savanna. And third, the proportion of fields with a single crop was much higher in the savanna and the savanna fringe, than in the forest and forest fringe. This appears to be related first to the need to maximize the return for the labour of clearance in forest, and second to the inherently poorer soils of much of the savanna. Furthermore in the

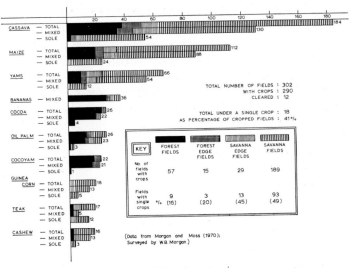

FIG. 9.

forest and its fringe the number of crops growing together in a single field was often 10 or 12, including three or more perennial tree crops. The labour requirement for clearing and weeding in forest (usually confined to the removal of woody seedlings and shoots from regenerating stools) also accounts in part for the concentration of annual food crops in the savanna. Where the proportion of forest land was low in a holding this tendency was even more pronounced. This clearly reveals a considerable degree of ecological perception on the part of the indigenous farmers, and a real consciousness of the differing potential and problems of the woody fallow areas in contrast to those with grassy fallow characteristics. In such a situa-

tion it is not at all surprising that care is taken to control fire where
it is likely to damage the more productive areas, namely the forest/
woody-fallow locations.

It is possible to suggest an idealized model for a typical forest
island in the area (Fig. 10). The core area of woody fallow is surrounded by a fringe area, often cultivated or planted with teak or
cashew; the distinction between forest fringe and savanna fringe
was made purely on the basis of the adventitious plants. This fringe
is usually characterized by somewhat better soils than the surrounding savanna, and often the microclimatic influence of the forest
extends into it in some measure. The island is surrounded by savanna
on the middle slopes, which in turn often gives place to gallery
forest along the watercourse. This gallery sometimes includes crops
similar to those found in the island on the summit and upper slope,
but more frequently is uncleared woodland.

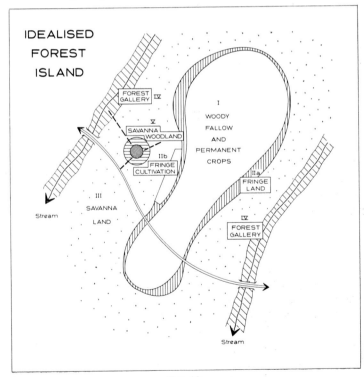

FIG. 10.

The kind of cropping pattern found in a holding in such a situation is illustrated in Fig. 11. This emphasizes the points made earlier concerning the implications of Fig. 9, and suggests that the generalizations tentatively made on the basis of the field survey in fact apply to individual holdings in themselves.

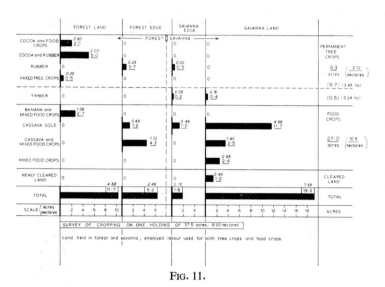

FIG. 11.

It is suggested therefore that this preliminary study of cropping patterns confirms strongly the notion that the indigenous farmers react perceptively to their economic environment, and utilize their biological resources so as to conserve them, rather than to exploit them destructively.

Conclusion

The more detailed work set out in this supplement to the original paper clearly supports the generalizations set out there. It is clear that understanding of the present pattern of forest/woody-fallow and savanna/grassy-fallow, together with their agricultural significance, can be achieved only by approaching the study of the plant groups present both from the standpoint of the edaphic and climatic factors in the detail of their spatial variability, and, simultaneously, from that of elucidating the patterns of husbandry systems and cropping patterns, with special reference to techniques of cultivation, including burning, which is an essential tool for most tropical cultivators. Such an approach must take into account varied motivations for using fire by indigenous farmers, together with their apparent awareness of its potential for the destruction of valued biological resources. Furthermore, the reasoning behind crop choice, and the locating of particular crops and crop combinations in relation to ecological and economic constraints needs to be more fully appreciated. Only on such a basis can agricultural development planning proceed on a secure foundation. And such a pattern of study would clearly be a significant contribution to the study of the ecology of human communities in the tropics.

Acknowledgements

I am grateful to the Centre of West African Studies in the University of Birmingham for the funds which made my study in western Nigeria possible; to the Research Fund of the University for the grant with which the aerial photographs were purchased; to the Director of Forest Research in Ibadan for permission to use the resources of the Forest Herbarium, and especially to Mr. D. P. Stanfield and Mr. Moses Latilo for their co-operation in the identification of the plant material, without which the study could never have been attempted; and to the Chief Agricultural Research Officer of the Western Region Ministry of Agriculture for the provision of trained labour and equipment for the setting out of the transects, and the taking of the soil samples.

References

BAEYENS, J. (1949) The bases of classification of tropical soils in relation to their agricultural value. *Commonwealth Bur. Soil Sci. Tech. Commn.*, **46**, 99–102.
BATCHELDER, R. B. and HIRT, H. A. (1966) *Fire in Tropical Forests and Grasslands*. (Natick Laboratories, Natick, Mass.).
LYR, H. and Hoffmann, G. (1967) Root growth in forest trees. *Int. Rev. For. Res.*, **2**, 181–237.
MORGAN, W. B. and MOSS, R. P. (1970) Farming, forest and savanna in Western Nigeria. *Erdkunde*.
NORRIS, J. M. and BARKHAM, J. B. (1968) Unpublished Ph.D. theses, University of Birmingham.
RODIN, L. E. and BAZILEVICH, N. I. (1967) *Production and Mineral Cycling in Terrestrial Vegetation* (trans. G. E. Fogg). (Oliver & Boyd: Edinburgh).
ROGERS, W. S. and HEAD, G. C. (1969) Factors affecting the distribution and growth of roots of perennial woody species. *Root Growth* (ed. W. J. WHITTINGTON) (Butterworths, London).

FORESTS AND THE DEVELOPMENT OF TROPICAL COUNTRIES

R. W. J. KEAY

CLEARING the forest has long been a first step in development. As man progressed from being a hunter and gatherer of his food, forests were cut to make room for crops and grazing animals, and later on for roads and railways and nearly every other manifestation of developed society. There is no doubt that the backwardness and poverty of the tropics is due in part to the luxuriance of the forests so much prized by the foresters, the ecologists and the conservationists who often find themselves at odds with the local people. The foresters' aim is often to grow fine trees for use as timber in 50 or more years time, while the people may well feel that their progress is being impeded by too many trees already. And yet all countries require some forest produce, and the most developed consume the most wood. It is therefore important to see the forests in the context of a general strategy for national development. When this is done it is usually evident that the forestry sector is capable of making a special contribution to economic growth.

Rural Population

It is all too easy to equate development with the growth of towns and the movement of people away from rural areas. So many modern visitors to tropical countries see little further beyond the towns than the airport, but if their jet should fly low enough, or if they should be obliged to make an internal flight in a small aircraft, they will see how much of the land below is still covered by farms, forests and wilderness. Indeed in many of the less developed tropical countries, over 70% of the population is rural and depends directly on the land for survival (Bunting, 1970).

I stress this point because it is often overlooked. The population explosion and the poverty of so many people in the tropical world are well enough known, and it has been too often assumed that the main emphasis in development must be on industrialization. Fortunately the inter-dependence of industrial and agricultural development is now more generally recognized. Development, if it is to occur at all must take place simultaneously in both industry and agriculture and in the infrastructure needed to sustain both (Lewis, 1970). Furthermore, it is now, somewhat belatedly, recognized that a high annual population growth rate, in countries where, say 80%, of the population is rural, will inevitably result in growing absolute numbers in the rural sector which even a high rate of migration to towns cannot at present absorb, and that rates of growth of wage-paid employment cannot keep pace with the growing labour force. It follows that the rural economy will have to generate more livelihoods (both self-employed and wage-paid) and to continue to do so for another 30 years at least (ODI, 1970).

Farm and Forest

The improvement of local agriculture, by the use of fertilizers, pesticides, new seeds, irrigation, etc., to meet the needs of rapidly growing populations is essentially a high priority in development. But in the tropical countries, bearing in mind the rural location of so much of the population, adequate and well distributed areas of forest must be retained or established to supply local needs, especially for firewood and building materials. With increasing use of electricity, solar energy and fossil fuels, dependence upon firewood becomes less, but it is unrealistic to imagine that these modern sources of energy will reach more than a small fraction of the vast rural populations for a long time.

Ideally the allocation of land between food crops, cash crops, forest and other uses, should be made on the basis of careful land-use surveys. Unfortunately this is rare in the tropics, and many countries have been seriously affected by unwise exploitation. One of the most serious problems is very widespread practice of shifting cultivation. Although acceptable at a primitive stage of a country's development, provided population density is low, shifting cultivation is unacceptable if a country wishes to advance, as most countries must, by improving agricultural production and by making the best use of forest resources. A recent FAO survey revealed that in Burma an estimated $31·5 million of timber was lost annually through shifting cultivation.

Water

Parallel to the development of agriculture must be the development and wise use of water resources. Rainfall in the inter-tropical countries varies from almost nil to the highest in the world, but in all, the storage and supply of water for domestic, agricultural and industrial use are vital for economic development. Rainfall in the tropics comes in the growing season when it exceeds evaporation and causes leaching in the soil. By contrast, in temperate regions crops draw on a reserve of water accumulated during the winter, and little leaching occurs during the growing season (Bunting, 1970). Furthermore, the concentration of rainfall in a few summer months and its sheer abundance in the wetter tropics leads to much more serious soil erosion than in temperate regions. It is, therefore, important to ensure that steep slopes, especially in river catchment areas, are properly protected; in most areas this means the preservation and proper management of forest.

Exports and Home Consumption

The wealth of tropical countries has traditionally come from exports of raw materials, but many of these have held their own in the world markets only because of low labour costs. When prices rise, there is strong pressure in the developed world to produce substitutes, either synthetic substances (e.g. man-made fibres instead of sisal) or locally grown crops (e.g. sugar beet instead of sugar cane). Great efforts have been made to improve productivity per man in certain tropical crops (e.g. rubber), but the export of unprocessed biological natural resources generally allows only a strictly limited increase in wealth.

Among tropical exports the place of timber is, however, interesting and special. There have been great changes over the past 40 years, with big increases in the amounts exported and a very substantial increase in the variety of species utilized.

Surveys by FAO indicate that the world's consumption of wood is increasing and is likely to continue increasing very substantially.

Contrary to popular ideas, consumption of wood does not decrease as incomes increase. The following table (FAO, 1967) showing annual consumption in different parts of the world illustrates this:

ANNUAL CONSUMPTION PER 1000 CAPITA (1963)

	North America	U.S.S.R.	Europe	Latin America	Asia/ Pacific	Africa
Sawn wood (m³)	481	439	172	52	35	12
Wood-based panels (m³)	93·7	12·2	23·1	2·7	1·9	0·8
Paper and paper board (metric tons)	189	17	55	12·2	6·8	2·9

The consumption of sawn wood in North America and in the Soviet Union is expected to fall slightly, but 30% increases by 1975 were forecast for Africa and Latin America. The expected increases in the consumption of wood-based panels (plywood, fibre board, particle board, etc.) and of wood pulp products are much greater than those for sawn wood. For instance the consumption per 1000 capita in North America of wood-based panels was 93·7 cubic metres in 1963 and were expected to reach 105 cubic metres in 1975, while that in Africa increased from 0·8 to 3. Total consumption of paper and paper board in North America was 189 metric tons per 1000 capitata in 1963 and was expected to reach 227·60 metric tons in 1975; comparable figures for Africa being 2·9 and 6·40. Figures for other regions lie between the extremes of Africa and North America.

The FAO Survey points out that the greater part of the additional wood requirements will come from the industrially advanced countries, but that "there is a very rapidly growing trade in wood from those developing countries endowed with large resources of tropical hardwood", and that "other developing countries are proving to be singularly well-favoured to establish low-cost, fast-growing, man-made forests which promise to become an increasingly important element of wood supply in the future".

The Director-General of FAO concluded that "The dynamic growth in markets for the woods that developing countries produce, or could produce, contrasts with the limited or poor market prospects facing most of their other primary agricultural products. Furthermore, trade in wood can often be relatively easily upgraded to trade in processed wood products and wood manufacture. The evaluation of the world wood sector thus offers unusually favourable opportunities for expansion in developing countries' exports—so necessary for adequate growth and development of their economies".

Industry

In the industrial development of a tropical country, forests and forest products have a crucial role with many strong links with the rest of the economy, "which in total are such that the sector's growth can have a dynamic propulsive effect on the development of the economy as a whole" (FAO, 1967).

Much has been written about the value of "intermediate technology": something between the traditional cottage industry and the large modern factory of the developed world. In the conversion of trees to sawn wood and other products there already exists a whole range of technology from the pit-saw (operated by two men, one above the log and the other below in a pit), through a variety of saw-benches to air-conditioned semi-automated factories producing plywood or paper. The industry can progress in stages and, according to location, there is still room for quite simple machinery.

Timber is vital to the construction industry, for housing (and there is plenty of room for improvement here), for industrial buildings and for a multitude of public works (e.g. bridges, culverts, railway sleepers, dams, etc.). And the more a country develops, the more wood it uses. With the level of consumption in the developing countries at present less than a tenth of that in developed countries, the prospect of expansion is enormous.

By the development of local timber industries, the more forested tropical countries can change from being net importers to being net exporters of sawn-timber and plywood. Furthermore, they can become self-sufficient in items such as window frames, doors and furniture, and may under favourable circumstances, be able to export manufactured or partly manufactured wooden items. Furniture factories are particularly suitable for the early stages of industrialization in tropical countries.

The local production of paper and other products from wood pulp presents many problems and requires a large investment, usually by an international industrial corporation. However, as the cost of importing paper may be substantial, there is much to be said for setting up pulp or paper mills of moderate size for the local market, as has been done in India and South America, using mixed tropical hardwoods. For larger mills and better quality paper, it is usually necessary to plant special forests, because the natural tropical forests are usually very mixed in their composition and the paper-making process requires wood of a special and uniform kind. The conditions for the rapid growth of selected broad-leaved trees (e.g. *Gmelina arborea*), as well as of certain conifers are so good in some tropical countries that it has been found worthwhile to create new forests (e.g. Swaziland).

This is but one example of the way in which rural forestry work (the planting, tending and harvesting of tree crops) has a vital part in the operation of integrated industrial enterprises whose later stages may include highly sophisticated technological processes.

Employment

The provision of useful jobs for a rapidly growing population, of whom more and more have gone to school and stayed there for increasingly longer periods, is a serious problem which all governments in tropical countries face or must soon face. Some of the new industrial projects provide rather few work places in relation to the high capital investment they require. For a tropical country which has plenty of labour, it is clearly sensible that only a part of its very limited capital resources should be used to establish capital intensive industries. For instance, if the country has $50 million for investment in industry and spends it on plant costing $5,000 per work place, a reasonable average for modern medium-scale industry, it would create only 10,000 work places. If, on the other hand, there was sufficient efficient manufacturing plant available at an average of $500 per work place, then 100,000 new jobs would be created (Blackett, 1969).

Very often the construction of a large industrial plant (e.g. an oil refinery) attracts a lot of labour, perhaps from rural to urban areas, but once built only employs a very small fraction of the force.

The employment provided by forestry and by industries using forest produce is, however, much more in tune with the needs of a developing tropical country. Work in the forests (felling, extracting, planting and tending) requires relatively little capital investment per work place; it provides a means of bringing money into remote rural areas and so does something to counteract the drift of people to the towns. Although plywood factories, pulping industries and large sawmills require considerable capital investment, a great deal of the timber conversion industry can properly be left to "intermediate technology" which requires small capital investment and provides a lot of work places.

Priorities in Forestry

If the forests are to make a full contribution to economic development, certain priorities must be observed. Firstly, adequate legal frameworks must be established and maintained. Forest laws may be unpopular, but when something is valuable, or potentially valuable, to a nation it is folly to allow it to be stolen, wasted or destroyed. Suitably selected areas for long-term forestry should be legally designated and steps taken to discourage waste in other areas. Secondly, research and development are needed to utilize as many as possible of the great variety of trees in the tropical forests. Considerable progress has been made in this direction in recent years; for instance, about 30 species of timber are now exported from Ghana, compared with only one (*Khaya ivorensis*) in most years before World War II.

Thirdly, as the forests are a renewable asset, it is important to find out how the more valuable trees can be regenerated, and to establish management plans to ensure a sustained yield. Much can be done in the natural or semi-natural forest, but with rapidly increasing populations and the consequent demand for more farmland, wood-production must come more and more from high-yielding plantations. This demands technical skill and capital, but the money spent will almost all go into the pockets of those in rural areas who clear the site and plant and tend the trees.

Finally, the role of forests in the economic development of a tropical country is not confined to timber production. Indeed, in the drier areas the forests, such as they are, can often most profitably be used for the grazing of domestic or wild animals to provide much needed protein, or as national parks to attract tourists. The protective value of forests on slopes, particularly in water catchment areas, has also to be taken into account even though it may be difficult to quantify in economic terms.

In terms of economic development, the tropical forests may quite properly be seen as a resource to be exploited, to provide employment and revenue and to save imports, and to be replaced in part by artificially created forests of fast growing useful species. However, it would be a great mistake economically, scientifically and aesthetically if adequate examples of natural forest were not conserved in all countries which have the good fortune of possessing these uniquely complex ecosystems.

Acknowledgments

I am glad to acknowledge the debt I owe to the late Lord Blackett and to Graham Jones for many stimulating discussions while Jones was writing his book *The Role of Science and Technology in Developing Countries* (1971).

References

BLACKETT (1969): *The Gap Widens.*
BUNTING, A. H. (1970): *Change in Agriculture.*
FAO (1967): *Wood—World Trends and Prospects.*
LEWIS, W. A. (1970): *The Development Process.*
Overseas Development Institute (1970): *Review – 4.*

TROPICAL HEALTH: A BROAD SURVEY

W. L. BARTON

HIPPOCRATES, in the fourth century B.C., was probably the first to describe the science of epidemiology, which, you recall, deals with the reasons for the causation of the prevalence of disease and the nature and causes of variations in it. In his treatise *Airs, Waters, Places* he stated that to investigate medicine properly one must take account of the seasons, the winds, water, orientation of the city, topography, and the customs and occupations of the people under observation (Hippocrates, 1939 edition).

Galen, in the second ceutury A.D., gave further guidance in stating that no cause [of disease] can be efficient without an aptitude of the body, observing that if the atmosphere carried seeds of pestilence a healthy body was less likely than the unhealthy one to be injured by them (Galen, 1951 edition).

From the earliest times, therefore, long befoıe the discoveries of Pasteur and Koch, men have been striving to replace the too-simple explanation of disease as a divine vengeance for wrongdoing or the result of an evil curse, by some more immediate cause. With the discoveries of bacteria towards the end of the last century the whole field of epidemiological investigation has broadened, and medical science has moved from the early "Empirical Era" when the emphasis was on the diagnosis and treatment of the sign and symptom of disease to the present "Era of Ecology".

Today, preoccupation is no longer with the disease entity, but rather with the study of the individual in his natural habitat. We are concerned with an understanding of man in relation to his total environment, social as well as physical, and emphasis is now directed towards the diagnosis and treatment of the community's ills (McGavran, 1956).

G

In considering tropical health, therefore, we have to study the pattern of disease as it affects whole communities, and so must take heed of the advice given by Hippocrates if we hope to give some explanation of the causes of the prevalence of disease in these tropical regions. When we speak of the tropical regions, of course, we have in mind particularly the areas in the New World, Africa, South-east Asia, and the Far East.

Addressing the Ninth Technical Meeting of the International Union for the Conservation of Nature, A. L. Adu, speaking on the subject The Ecology of Man in a Tropical Environment, stated that "the special problems of the tropics are associated with the fact that we have a particularly delicate relationship with the physical factors of climate, soil, and the natural biological community that has become established. This balance is very easily upset, and any major disturbance is likely to be disastrous" (Int. Un. Conservatn. Nature, 1964). Any of us who have lived or worked in these areas will, I am sure, readily agree with these words, and they can certainly be well demonstrated in certain disease patterns occurring in these regions.

The first consideration in our survey must be with the demographic picture of the populations or communities. There are throughout the regions enormous variations in the size and density of populations, with no common pattern emerging. Population sizes range from around a million in a large country like Botswana, to over 120 million in Indonesia, but it is the density of populations in these countries that is of greater significance. Again we meet a wide range; for example there are 5 per square km in the Congo, 10 in Tanzania, 39 in Nigeria, rising to 232 per square km in Taiwan, and over 390 per square km in Java. All the different communities in their varying densities live in a reasonable state of biological balance with their environment. This state of equilibrium in most of the tropical areas is determined by the laws of nature and maintained by certain factors which we might like to call the density dependent factors. We see in nature that the maintenance of the number of the species is the end result of conflict between two opposing forces—on the one hand the production of more offspring than can hope to survive, and on the other the constant destruction of individuals directly by traumatic or infective causes, or indirectly by nutritional factors (Burnett, 1962).

One could devote the whole of this survey to malaria, showing how and why it demonstrates variations in pattern throughout the whole tropical region. However, there are other conditions which are of great significance in these areas, and which also demonstrate variations in patterns. One such disease is onchocerciasis, which affects the African savanna belt south of the Sahara, and is also seen in Guatemala, Mexico, Colombia, and Venezuela. This disease, attributed to a filarial worm is transmitted by a small, black fly, *Simulium*, and is responsible for blindness of up to 10% of the population in these regions, and as a result renders large areas of the country uninhabitable (Hunter, 1966). The fly breeds in flowing rivers and an essential requirement for its development is a high oxygen content in the water. Dependent on the size of the river in which the breeding takes place and the degree of shade and shelter of the river bank, there can be different optimum breeding seasons. It would be optimum in the large rivers when the flow is low and the rocks become exposed, and therefore churn up the water and oxygenate it, while in the small rivers the optimum season would be immediately following the onset of rains when the fast-flowing narrow rivers are "bubbling" with the flow. Though the disease may have a seasonal peak of transmission, it is a disease of chronic and crippling nature through the blindness that it causes.

Particular reference to trypanosomiasis and schistosomiasis is made in other chapters, and will demonstrate the different patterns of disease that can result from variations in the parasite.

When one has said all there is to say about animal reservoirs, the characteristics of protozoal and parasitic infections, the direct and indirect effects of climate, it is still true to say that human disease is a function of human behaviour, particularly of community or crowd behaviour (Smith, 1941), and no survey of health, as it may affect these or any other regions, would be complete without reference to the way in which culture can affect disease. A community's cultural and behaviour patterns can encourage or minimize the transmission of disease indirectly, through the type of house that they build and live in, the distribution of the family in the various rooms throughout the house, the clothes that they wear or the lack of them, the diet, and customs related to feeding. All these can be dictated by general tribal or religious beliefs and customs. Changes in customs and habits do occur, but seldom in developing communities are such changes motivated for health reasons. Nevertheless, however, they can have a specific effect on health. Again, changes in the population itself can affect the disease picture. Major changes in host population have taken place in the Fijis, Mauritius, and, of course, the New World. Not only do these changes in the population introduce new diseases which can sweep through a whole community, for example venereal disease, tuberculosis, and yellow fever, but they often result in changes in cultural habits, which in turn bring about changes in environment and consequently in disease patterns (May, 1958). Finally, the attitudes of communities to health and disease can have a direct effect on the success of a health programme (Paul, 1955).

I have attempted to give a brief survey of tropical health and to indicate by a few examples the delicate relationship between health aspects of a community and various environmental factors. You will appreciate that a major function of tropical hygiene is to maintain a proper balance between the prevention of those conditions that dominate the health picture of a community and the development of sociological and educational activities within general health services, all with proper attention to the demographic consequences of improved health (Macdonald, 1965).

References

ALLISON, A. C. (1954) *Brit. Med. J.*, **i**, 290.
BURNETT, F. M. (1962) *Natural History of Infectious Disease*, 3rd edn., Cambridge University Press, Cambridge.
GALEN (1951 edn.) *A Translation of Galen's Hygiene* by R. M. GREEN, Thomas, Springfield.
HIPPOCRATES (1939 edn.) *Airs, Waters, Places*, vol. I of Hippocrates, Heinemann, London.
HUNTER, J. M. (1966) *Geog. Rev.*, **56**, 398.
INT. UNION CONSERV. NATURE (1964) *I.U.C.N. Publs.* N.S. 4, Morges, Switzerland.
MACDONALD, G. (1965) *Trans. Roy. Soc. Trop. Med. Hyg.*, **59**, 611.
MAY, J. M. (1958) *The Ecology of Human Disease*, American Geographical Society: Studies in Medical Geography, **1**, MD Publ., New York.
MCGAVRAN, E. G. (1956) *J. Amer. Med. Assoc.*, **162**, 723.
PAUL, B. D. (1955) (Ed.) *Health, Culture and Community*, Russell Sage Foundation, New York.
SMITH, G. (1941) *Plague on Us*, Commonwealth Fund.

PHYSIOLOGICAL REACTIONS TO HEAT IN MAN

D. L. INGRAM

MAN is committed to keeping the temperature of the body core within fairly narrow limits, and almost any environment provides some problems associated with heat balance. These problems can be summed up in the form of a simple equation which applies to all homeotherms:

$$M = E \pm R \pm C \pm K \pm S \qquad (1)$$

M is the heat produced by metabolism and varies according to whether the subject is working or resting and also with the time which has elapsed since the last meal. E is the loss of heat by the evaporation of moisture from the skin and the respiratory tract. R, C and K are the heat exchanges by radiation, convection and conduction, respectively, and any of these can be positive or negative. Thus under conditions of high solar radiation there may be a net gain of heat by radiation, and when air temperature is above skin temperature the body gains heat by convection. S is any alteration in the heat content of the body and appears as a change in mean body temperature. This equation must always balance and under extremely hot conditions S becomes progressively greater until the animal dies from overheating (hyperthermia). This general subject of man and animals in hot environments has recently been reviewed by Ingram and Mount (1975).

The mechanisms by which heat balance is achieved fall into three classes: (1) morphological, (2) autonomic, (3) behavioural. In man the chief variable morphological feature which influences heat balance in a hot climate is the colour of the skin which is of some significance with respect to solar radiation.

95

Differences in body conformation with respect to the amount of fat and the length of the limbs are probably also of some consequence, but the subject has not received much systematic attention. The autonomic mechanisms include the control of metabolic rate, vasomotor tone and sweating, the last of which is highly developed in man. Behavioural patterns which include the building of shelters and the wearing of clothes are employed by all groups of people to some extent, and in highly developed societies they can make man completely independent of the general environment.

The features outlined in the above classes may be partly under genetic control, but some adaptation can occur within the individual and this is of considerable importance in man's tolerance of a hot environment. There are thus two groups of people to be considered: those born in warm countries and already acclimatized, and those who move there from temperate climates.

The tropics are associated with high ambient temperatures for at least part of the day, often in combination with intense solar radiation, so that the potential for heat loss by convection and radiation is considerably reduced or even abolished. Under these conditions the evaporation of water becomes of great importance since it is the only channel by which significant amounts of heat can be lost, and factors which limit moisture vaporization, such as high humidity, become important. In a hot humid climate the control of body temperature can be much more difficult than in a hot dry one, although in the latter case a difficulty in obtaining drinking water may lead to serious problems of dehydration. Not all tropical regions, however, are uniformly hot. Deserts frequently provide the dual hazards of a high solar heat load by day combined with a considerable drop in temperature at night which involve animals in alternate problems of heat loss and heat conservation.

Evaporative Heat Loss

A certain minimum quantity of water, depending on the environmental conditions, is always lost from the respiratory tract and through the skin. These channels of evaporation can be considerably increased, and controlled by the mechanisms of panting and sweating. Man does not pant, but his sweating mechanism is much more highly developed than in other animals and his potential for dissipating heat by evaporation is quite considerable and equivalent to 20 times his resting metabolic rate. At the maximum a man may lose in excess of 3 kg. of water per hour, and although this rate cannot be kept up for long periods, he can nevertheless maintain a loss of 10–12 kg. per day. This high rate of sweating makes him very tolerant of heat as was demonstrated many years ago by Blagden (1774, 1775) who took a dog and a piece of raw meat with him into a room at over 100°C and remained there long enough for the meat to be cooked although he and the dog came to no harm.

The production of sweat in man depends on the functions of eccrine (atrichial) glands in contrast to other sweating mammals, such as the cow, which have apocrine (epitrichial) glands. The mechanisms by which these types of gland function have been considered by Kuno (1956) and Bligh (1967) and the general subject of sweating has been reviewed by Weiner and Hellman (1960). Eccrine glands are present all over the body surface, but reach the highest density of 2000 per sq. cm. on the palm of the hand and the sole of the foot, but paradoxically in neither place do they play a part in thermoregulation. The glands which help to regulate body temperature occur at the much lower densities of 200–300 per sq. cm. on the face and 100–200 per sq. cm. on the trunk and limbs. On exposure to a hot environment sweating begins on the lower half of the body, starting on the foot and extending upwards appearing last on the head and forearm. Initially the rate of sweat production is low, but if body temperature continues to rise the number of glands producing sweat within a given area increases, leading to an overall increase in moisture vaporization. With still further heating there is finally an increase in the quantity of sweat produced by each gland in unit time.

The level at which the rate of sweating reaches a plateau depends on several factors and although attempts have been made to relate it to a single variable, such as core temperature, this has proved to be impossible for the whole range of conditions to which man is exposed (Kerslake, 1972). In warm environments exercise leads to hyperthermia, so that for a given rate of work sweat rate is closely related to core temperature, and it is in men working at high ambient temperatures that the highest rates of sweating are observed. Women follow a similar pattern to men, but for a given set of conditions they have a lower rate of moisture loss.

Continuous exposure to a hot climate, as for example living in the desert, leads to an improvement in heat tolerance which is most obvious during the first four days (Adolph, 1947). This change is due, partly, to the improved ability to sweat, the secretion of the glands becoming more dilute and more copious. Studies in the laboratory have shown that short daily exposures to heat over about 2 weeks can also lead to an improved ability to sweat and this finding has led to considerable interest with respect to artificial acclimatization (Fox, 1974). Two methods have been employed. In the first men were exposed to a hot environment and required to work at a fixed rate for 100 min. per day. Sweat rates increased rapidly over the first 4 or 5 days and then more slowly up to about the tenth day when a plateau was reached. The increased ability to sweat was found to depend not only on the environmental temperature but also on the rate of work performed during the exposure and hence a further improvement could be achieved by increasing the amount of physical exercise. Increasing the length of exposure beyond 100 min, or using two training periods per day, did not increase the rate, or the degree of adaptation. In addition to increasing the rate of moisture vaporization it was found that after adaptation sweating began sooner after the onset of exposure to heat, and at a lower body temperature. The second and more recent method of acclimatizing men artificially to a hot environment has involved the use of controlled hyperthermia. The subject sits in a room at body temperature and is dressed in a plastic suit which is ventilated by a stream of hot humid air. Under these conditions core temperature increases and can be controlled at an elevated level by periodically passing dry air through the suit to allow evaporative heat loss. In control engineering terms the system acts as an "open loop" since no matter how much the man sweats body temperature remains elevated. Under these conditions the increase in the ability to sweat is related both to the core temperature and the duration of exposure. Unlike the previous method in which the rate of improvement began to level off after 4 or 5 days, in the second situation the rate of sweating increased linearly over 12 days and reached as much as three times the value before acclimatization.

Men may also become acclimatized "naturally" by being exposed to a hot climate, but the rate at which this occurs is difficult to estimate because it is rarely possible to use properly controlled conditions. Nevertheless, it appears that Nigerian farmers who do fairly hard manual work do not reach the physiological limit of acclimatization to heat: by contrast it is doubtful if South African goldminers could become further adapted. After removal from a hot climate, or stopping exercise, there may be an initial rapid decline in the degree of acclimatization, with a further fall over the next two or three weeks. There is some evidence that the rate of reacclimatization may be more rapid than in controls subjected to heat for the first time. Evidence for the idea that different races have different potentials for acclimatization is equivocal.

The complex nature of the mechanisms which control the amount of sweating can be illustrated by reference to just a few experiments. In the studies using controlled hyperthermia it was possible to demonstrate that a rise in temperature alone was sufficient to improve the ability to sweat, since an increased rate of sweat production could be induced even during treatments in which the loss of liquid from the gland was prevented (Fox, 1974). On the other hand treatment of an area of skin with drugs which induce the expulsion of sweat in the absence of heating can also lead to an enhanced rate of moisture vaporization from the skin when the subject is exposed to a hot environment. This local nature of the adaptation process is also illustrated by the fact that it is possible to acclimatize one limb alone by immersing it in a bath of hot water while the rest of the body is exposed to cool conditions.

The production of an increased quantity of sweat is not sufficient to ensure cooling of the body; the physical conditions for moisture vaporization also need to be favourable. The factors involved in limiting the loss of water by evaporation have been reviewed by Kerslake (1972), Monteith (1973) and Ingram and Mount (1975). The latent heat of vaporization of water varies slightly according to the temperature at which it is evaporated, from 2501 J/gm at 0°C to 2406 J/gm at 40°C and in the tropics it is obviously the latter figure which is relevant. The extent to which the body can be cooled by this latent heat depends on two factors. One is the amount of water vapour already present in the air; the other is the extent to which the latent heat is derived from the body rather than the ambient air. For example moisture which evaporated from the surface of clothing, could derive at least some of its latent heat from the environment rather than the body with the result that the efficiency of sweating would be much reduced.

When water evaporates into a fixed quantity of air the concentration of vapour increases to a maximum which is known as the saturation vapour pressure. This maximum pressure depends on the temperature and increases in a non-linear fashion so that the quantity of additional water which can evaporate into a fixed volume of air when the temperature increases from 39° to 40°C is about five times as great as when the temperature increases from 1° to 2°C. The ratio of the saturation vapour pressure to the actual vapour pressure is the relative humidity and indicates the capacity of the air to take up additional vapour. Because the saturation vapour pressure increases as temperature rises the relative humidity by itself is of limited help in estimating the potential for evaporative heat loss because a relative humidity of 80% at 2°C would leave very little room for additional vapour, while at 40°C the capacity would be quite large. In practice a comparison between the wet bulb (W.B.) temperature, i.e. the temperature of a thermometer on which the bulb is covered with a wet wick, and the dry bulb (D.B.) temperature, i.e. a thermometer with no wick, gives the information which is required. The closer W.B. is to the D.B. temperature, the lower is the evaporation potential, and when the W.B. and D.B. have the same reading the air is saturated.

When a man sweats the space into which the moisture evaporates is that in contact with the skin and the W.B. and D.B. temperatures in this region may not be the same as the general ambient air. A man wearing fairly closely fitting clothes may rapidly approach the condition where his skin is in contact with air which is at the saturation vapour pressure, even though the general ambient air is below it. Loose fitting robes such as those worn by desert people on the other hand allow free exchange of air within the clothing especially if there is a breeze. A naked man is best placed to evaporate water particularly if air movement is high, but under conditions of high solar radiation he will encounter an additional heat load. The ideal clothing will depend on the environmental conditions and the load of physical work. For a man resting under a high solar heat load loose fitting clothes are best, but a man doing hard physical work under the same conditions is best with no clothing.

Another component of evaporative heat transfer that has received attention in the past is the energy required to expand water vapour from near saturation pressure close to the skin, to the vapour pressure of the ambient air. The expansion of the vapour requires energy as does any expanding gas and there must therefore be a fall in temperature somewhere in the system. In practice, particularly when the skin is wet, the necessary energy appears to be derived mainly from the ambient air rather than the skin and does not contribute, significantly, to cooling the body (Kerslake, 1972).

A further factor which contributes to the efficiency of sweating is the extent to which the surface of the body is wetted. Clearly for maximum heat transfer all the skin should be wet, but any perspiration which drips off the body does not contribute to evaporative heat loss. Even liquid sweat taken up by clothing has a reduced efficiency in cooling the body as discussed above. Conversely areas of dry skin make no contribution. The perfect equilibrium state in which the skin remains uniformly wet with no loss by sweat running off the body hardly ever occurs, and for a consideration of the problems this raises in calculating the evaporation heat loss the reader is referred to Kerslake (1972).

Problems of Dehydration

The loss of large quantities of water by sweating threatens the body with dehydration and because sweat contains salt there is also a danger that the electrolyte balance can be disturbed. On initial exposure to heat the sweat is relatively concentrated so that water and electrolytes are lost at the same rate with the result that there is little or no disturbance to the osmotic balance. As a consequence in spite of the loss of water, the subject does not feel unduly thirsty and is liable to undergo some degree of voluntary dehydration. After a period of adaptation the sweat becomes more dilute and the thirst mechanism is activated so that water balance is more nearly maintained. Nevertheless there is a lag between water loss and thirst and if a man works hard in a hot environment he may simply be unable to drink water fast enough to maintain a balance. Attempts by men to force themselves to drink sufficient water may actually lead to vomiting. This phenomenon has been considered by Schmidt-Nielsen (1964) who points out that the problem is not fully understood, but suggests that it is probably related to the fact that the factors which influence thirst are complex and involve inputs from several sources.

In the absence of water, signs of thirst soon appear and are very strong even at 2% of water loss, although they do not become progressively more severe. In contrast to some other animals dehydration involves man in a relatively greater loss of water from the plasma than from the tissues; the reason for this is not clear, but it is unlikely to be due to a rate limiting factor in the transfer of water from the tissues since man can easily lose more water than his entire blood volume during one day. An important consequence of this loss of plasma water is that the blood becomes more viscous and there is therefore a concomitant extra work load on the heart at a time when rapid circulation of blood is needed to transfer heat from the body core to the surface. Mechanisms which compensate for the loss of water through sweating are thus of considerable significance and one obvious economy is in the reduction of urine volume in a hot climate to about half that observed in a temperate one. Under conditions of severe dehydration the volume falls even further, but man's ability to produce a concentrated urine is very limited and falls far short of that exhibited by animals such as the camel. The restricted capacity to concentrate urine also imposes constraints on the electrolyte content of water which can usefully be drunk. The drinking of concentrated urine by men stranded in the desert is completely useless because the salts it contains require exactly the same amount of water for their subsequent excretion. Fluid with an even higher salt content would require an even greater volume of water for excretion than that which was drunk. On the other hand because of the loss of salt in the sweat a slightly saline water cannot only be tolerated, but is desirable in order to avoid the depletion of electrolytes from the body.

Schmidt-Nielsen (1964) has considered the value of various tactics for men about to undertake a journey to the desert, and the possible advantage of drinking large quantities of water. He concludes that very little can be done by way of preparation because any excess of water over immediate requirements simply leads to a diuresis. Some advantage may be gained if the water contains a little salt which maintains the osmotic balance in the body, but the extent to which survival time could be prolonged is very limited. Certainly no amount of training can result in a substantial reduction in the use of water and any saving which does occur is as the result of behavioural changes rather than alterations in the autonomic system. Even after quite pronounced dehydration the sweat rate has very little tendency to diminish, and although dehydrated men use rather less water than controls the difference seems to be related to an economy of work effort on the part of men deprived of water.

The Cardiovascular System

The cardiovascular system performs two functions which are of particular significance for thermoregulation in man. One is that it transports heat from deep in the body to the skin where it can be lost to the environment; the other is that it transports water to the sweat glands. The rate at which sensible (non-evaporative) heat is lost from the body core is proportional to the temperature gradient between core and the environment and to the thermal conductance of the peripheral tissues particularly those of the limbs. When blood flow in the peripheral tissue is high, skin temperature comes closer to core temperature and the tissue conductance is thus increased. Within that range of ambient temperatures which is above the critical temperature (i.e. the temperature below which metabolism must increase in order to keep the body temperature constant and which is 28°C for a nude man), but below the point at which sweating starts, thermal balance is under only vaso-motor control. The range of ambient conditions in which heat loss can be controlled purely by peripheral blood flow depends on the amount of clothing, the degree of physical work, air movement and the extent of the solar radiation; but the D.B. temperatures are likely to be about 25°C. In ambient conditions such as these very little demand is made on the body's material resources such as food or water and problems associated with heat balance are at a minimum. At high environmental temperatures the gradient available for the loss of heat, decreases, and during hard physical work the quantity of heat to be lost increases. These conditions induce sweating and involve the diversion of large amounts of blood to the periphery which leads to an increase in the vascular space. This is to some extent offset by vasoconstriction in other regions such as the kidney, but compensation is by no means complete. In addition as already mentioned there is a dehydration on first exposure to heat which particularly affects the plasma. The net result is that the cardiovascular system is under strain and this manifests itself in a tendency towards fainting particularly if the

H

subject stands up suddenly after lying down. After a period of acclimatization especially when it is associated with exercise, the blood volume increases by about 10% provided water is readily available and the tendency towards fainting is much reduced. The exposure to hot conditions also involves an increase in cardiac output which may be as high as $15l \ min^{-1}$ (Hertzman, 1959). This increase is more than can be accounted for on the basis of an increased blood flow in the skin, and suggests that the rate of flow in other parts of the body may also increase in a hot environment.

The control of vasomotor tone is effected by two systems in man. One is the release of vasoconstriction which occurs all over the body on exposure to heat (with the exception of the forehead where there is no constrictor tone). This system is similar to that seen in other mammals, but man has an additional mechanism which brings about a further "active" vasodilation in the limbs. The substance responsible for the greater release of vasomotor tone is bradykinin which is produced by the sweat glands. The fact that such a substance has been evolved underlines the importance of a high blood flow in an animal capable of producing the large amounts of sweat seen in man.

Tropical regions may experience wide fluctuations in the thermal environment and when the ambient temperature falls heat loss must be reduced. In man this is frequently assisted by the use of clothes, shelter and fires, but the insulation of the body tissues themselves can be increased by vasoconstriction. This occurs chiefly in the limbs where in addition to vasoconstriction in the skin, the cool venous blood is diverted to vessels which pass close to the arterial blood. Under these conditions a heat exchanger system operates and heat from the arterial blood is transferred to the venous blood, conserving heat at the same time as supplying the limbs with blood. The volume taken up by the body core is contracted and the lower part of the limbs are maintained at a lower temperature. This process along with the ability to sleep while shivering plays a part in helping people such as the Kalahari bushmen who use no clothing to survive during the desert night.

Metabolism and the Endocrine System

The role of hormones in adaptation to hot environments has recently been reviewed by Collins and Weiner (1968). The metabolic rate is increased by thyroxine and there is some evidence in man that the activity of the thyroid gland is reduced during prolonged exposure to heat. There is however a considerable amount of variation between individuals and this may account for the fact that some investigators have not found any difference in metabolism or thyroid activity in men exposed to heat.

The hormones of the adrenal medulla are concerned with metabolism; they are involved in the response of the body to cold rather than heat and there appears to be no evidence that circulating levels differ in men exposed to hot environments. The glucocorticoids do however decrease in men after exposure to the heat and may play a part in any decreased metabolic rate. Alternatively the decrease in the level of glucocorticoids may be related in some way to their effect on electrolytes.

A second aspect of the role of hormones during heat exposure is in connection with mineral and water metabolism. Exposure to a hot environment is associated with an increase in the excretion of aldosterone, which is the principal mineralocorticoid, in the urine. The mechanisms by which this occurs are not however clear and it may be that it depends not on heat exposure but on the extent to which osmotic equilibrium is disturbed, since in some studies in which salt and water balance were maintained there was no change in aldosterone. Other studies have, however, demonstrated an increase in the quantity of aldosterone in the urine during the summer. The effect of this increased level of mineralocorticoid is to reduce not only sodium loss by the kidney, but also the sodium concentration of sweat.

The reduction in urine flow on initial exposure to heat is probably due chiefly to a fall in renal blood flow and the consequent reduction in glomerular filtration rate. The sustained reduction is related to the secretion of antidiuretic hormone (ADH) by the pituitary gland. The level of ADH in the blood tends to be higher during exposure to heat even when the subject is in water balance, and the increase in ADH on exposure to heat is greater in summer than in winter. Again the mechanisms by which these changes are controlled are not yet clear but there appears to be an interaction between the effects of temperature and the availability of water.

Radiant Heat

For a full account of the physics of radiant heat exchange in biological systems the reader is referred to Monteith (1973) and some comparative aspects of the effects of solar radiation are dealt with by Ingram and Mount (1976). The wavelength at which an object gives off radiant heat depends on its temperature and for the sun with a surface temperature in the region of 6000°K the spectrum is $0.3\,\mu$m to $3\,\mu$m and is termed short-wave radiation. Objects on the earth such as soil, rocks, animals and plants have very much lower temperatures and the wave lengths they emit cover a quite different spectrum with a peak at $10\,\mu$m, i.e. long-wave radiation. The radiant exchange between the earth and the sun is for all practical purposes one way only; it may reach an object directly, or it may be scattered by water vapour and clouds, or it may be reflected off nearby objects. The reflectivity of soil and rocks is very variable, being high for white surfaces and low for dark ones. The long-wave radiation on the other hand must be treated as an exchange of energy between two surfaces such as skin and a nearby rock. The net amount of radiant energy received by the cooler object is proportional to the difference in the fourth power of their absolute temperatures and the emissivities of the surfaces. Where both emissivities are close to unity the relation is given by the formula:

$$H = \sigma A (T_1^4 - T_2^4) \qquad (2)$$

Where H is the energy exchange, A is the area of the surfaces, σ is the Stephen-Boltzman constant and T_1 and T_2 are the temperatures in °K. A highly polished surface has a low emissivity, but most naturally occurring materials such as rocks, and skin, have values for emissivity close to unity at wavelengths greater than $5\,\mu$m.

The amount of solar radiation reaching the outer atmosphere is estimated to be 1360 W.m^{-2} and of this up to 1000 W.m^{-2} may reach the surface of the earth in some tropical regions (Monteith, 1973). The rate at which heat is lost from a man at rest in a thermally neutral environment is about 50 W.m^{-2} and it will therefore be appreciated that the effects of solar radiation are potentially very significant for heat balance. The whole surface area of the body is not of course exposed to the sun but even those parts which are in the shade will receive some reflected short-wave radiation in addition to long-wave radiation given off from rocks and the soil. The problem of radiant heat exchange in man and animals has been reviewed by Cena (1974) who describes the net amount of radiation received as follows:

Net radiation $(R_n) = (1-p^*)(St+Se) + E(Ld+Le) - L_b$ (3)

St = the total direct and diffuse solar radiation.

Se = short wave radiation reflected from the earth.

p^* = the short wave reflection coefficient of the human body Ld, Le and L_b are the long-wave radiative fluxes from the atmosphere the earth and the body, respectively. E is the emissivity of the skin.

The term $(St+Se)$ is influenced by the posture taken up by the subject with respect to the sun and the altitude of the sun. Underwood and Ward (1966) have studied this problem and derived a formula for calculating the surface area exposed to direct radiation from photographs of the body's silhouette taken from various angles of altitude and azimuth. From this work and from common experience it is obvious that a man can influence the degree of solar heat load quite considerably simply by his behaviour in orientation to the sun.

The term $(1-p^*)$ is determined by the colour of the skin, or clothing. A black surface absorbs nearly all the solar radiation while a white skin will reflect about half. For a naked man this raises a paradox since the dark skin associated with people in the tropics would appear to be a disadvantage with respect to heat load. Further examination, however, reveals that a black skin absorbs heat in the superficial layers from where it can readily be lost again by convection, while radiation penetrates much deeper into white skin where heat may be carried into the body core by the blood. In addition pigmented skin offers some protection from the harmful effects of ultra violet radiation. The question of colour is also of importance with respect to clothing. A white cloth would appear at first consideration to have the advantage, but in fact desert peoples use both black and white robes. These robes are usually loose fitting and allow plenty of air movement to ventilate the skin surface and so do not form a barrier to moderate rates of sweating. A black robe will absorb the solar radiation on the surface from where it can be lost again by convection assisted by the desert breezes. The robe's surface temperature will, however, be high and the skin will therefore receive an additional heat load from long-wave radiation. A white robe would certainly reflect more solar radiation while it was clean but it may well be more translucent than black cloth and so allow some radiation to reach the skin and produce undesirable heating. The fact that both types of clothing are used suggests that in practice neither has a very considerable advantage over the other. The important thing is that the robe should be loose and flowing thus allowing the transport of water vapour while pioviding protection from radiation. For a man working at a rate of more than 280 W.m^{-2}, however, clothing hinders evaporation too much and any shelter from the sun would best be provided by a canopy.

Burton and Edholm (1955) derived a method for treating the solar heat load so that it could be regarded as a "thermal radiation increment", or the amount by which the dry bulb temperature would have to be increased to produce an equivalent environment in the absence of a solar load. Thus the difference in temperature between the skin and the clothing $(T_s - T_{cl})$ is found from HI_{cl}, where H is the heat loss per unit area from the skin and I_{cl} is the insulation of the clothes in °C per unit of heat loss. The temperature gradient between the clothes and the ambient air is $(T_{cl} - T_a)$ and is given by $(H+R)I_a$ where R is the solar radiation per unit area and I_a the insulation of the boundary layer of air.

$$T_s - T_a = HI_{cl} + (H+R)I_a \qquad (4)$$

$$= H(I_{cl} + I_a) + RI_a \qquad (5)$$

RI_a is the radiation increment. In still air when I_a is large then for a given value of R the increment will be greater than in a breeze when I_a will be reduced. If equation (4) is divided throughout by $(I_{cl} + I_a)$ we get:

$$\frac{T_s - T_a}{I_{cl} + I_a} = H + R \frac{I_a}{I_{cl} + I_a} \qquad (6)$$

The efficiency with which the solar load is added to the body's metabolism is thus modified by the insulation of the air divided by the total insulation. Again in a breeze when I_a is reduced, the effect of the solar load is reduced, but by contrast when the insulation of the clothes is reduced the effect of the solar load is increased.

Heat Tolerance

It is of practical importance to obtain some estimate of the heat tolerance of human subjects and to assess the strain produced in the body by various types of thermal stress imposed by the environment. Such measurements are of use in indicating the extent to which specific tasks can be undertaken in a given environment and also in making comparisons between different kinds of hot climate, e.g. in determining what sort of hot dry climate produces the same effects on the body as a given hot wet climate. The subject has been very fully examined by Kerslake (1972) and the following is only a brief summary of the material available.

One of the first attempts to predict the severity of the stress represented by a particular set of environmental conditions was made by Haldane (1905) who was concerned with circumstances in which there was no solar radiation. He used the W.B. temperature and because man relies so much on sweating this single parameter proved to be a much better indicator of stress than the D.B. temperature. In addition it appears that a hot wet atmosphere is subjectively much more unpleasant than a hot dry one which produces very much the same autonomic thermoregulatory responses. Since Haldane there have been many other investigations, and systems have been devised which take into account more components of the environment. In the system proposed by Hatch (1963) the strain is estimated from the ratio of cutaneous blood flow to cardiac output, and the stress is estimated from the rate of sweating. It is obviously reasonable to use physiological responses to measure strain because this is produced in the organism, but to use such responses to measure stress involves some difficulties. Thus as already mentioned the sweating response changes with the degree of acclimatization and it could appear that the stress of the same environment varied with time. On the other hand if due attention is paid to this limitation it is found that the index is useful because the body is very efficient at integrating the various parameters of the environment and weighting them correctly with respect to man. Heat tolerance has also been measured by using the Predicted Four Hour Sweat Rate (P4SR). This is based on measurement made on healthy young men exposed to a given set of conditions in two different sets of clothing. Other systems use some sort of ratio between the maximum possible rate of sweating, and the rate of sweating required to achieve equilibrium. A method which has been used by the armed services in training men for service in hot climates is based on the W.B. temperature and the temperature of the globe thermometer (WBGT). This last system takes into account both the humidity and the radiant temperature and has the advantage of being readily determined.

Heat Illnesses

The diseases associated with hot climates and heat exposure have been reviewed by Leithead and Lind (1964). The tendency to fainting on exposure to heat and the problem of dehydration have already been mentioned. In addition a man with a high rate of sweating may also suffer nausea and the complaint known as miner's cramp. These last symptoms are associated with the depletion of electrolytes and can be alleviated by taking salt tablets with the drinking water. Prolonged sweating can also affect the sweat glands and lead to a tingling sensation in the skin known as prickly heat. In addition exposure to heat may involve psychological changes which result in a decline in the performance of skilled operations. It is, however, the drive or motivation which is affected rather than the actual capacity to work.

Heat stroke, sometimes called sun stroke, occurs as the result of a breakdown in the thermoregulatory system, and the hyperpyrexia which results when sweating fails may be fatal.

Comparative Physiology of Heat Exposure

The physiological reactions to heat dealt with so far apply to man and it must not be assumed that other species behave in the same way. The subject of the reactions of man and animals to hot environments has received attention by Ingram and Mount (1975), but it may be useful to comment here on some of the animals which are associated with man.

The dog is capable of a high evaporative heat loss by panting, but not by sweating; consequently it may tolerate a given environment as well as man, but the effects of heat exposure will not be the same. For example there is no loss of electrolytes in panting provided the animal does not drool saliva, but there are changes in blood PCO_2 with over ventilation. The camel which has a legendary tolerance of heat owes much to its large size which bestows a big capacity to store heat during the day and lose it again at night. This is combined with the ability to accept large fluctuations in core temperature which increases its heat storage capacity even further. The merino sheep tolerates high levels of solar radiation by virtue of its thick fleece, while some desert rodents simply become nocturnal and spend the daytime in a burrow. The very different effects that the same environment may have on different species can perhaps best be summarized by reference to the relative weighting which must be given to the W.B. and D.B. temperatures in order to arrive at an effective temperature for man, cattle and pigs. These are, respectively: 85% W.B.+15% D.B., 65% W.B.+35% D.B., and 35%W.B.+65% D.B.

References

ADOLPH, E. F. (1947) *Physiology of Man in the Desert*. Interscience, New York.
BLAGDEN, C. (1774) Experiments and observations in an heated room. *Phil. Trans. Roy. Soc.*, **65**, 111–123.
BLAGDEN, C. (1775) Further experiments and observations in an heated room. *Phil. Trans. Roy. Soc.*, **65**, 484–494.
BLIGH, J. (1967) A thesis concerning the processes of secretion and discharge of sweat. *Environ. Res.*, **1**, 28–45.
BURTON, A. C. and EDHOLM, O. G. (1955) *Man in a Cold Environment*. Edward Arnold, London.
CENA, K. (1974) Radiative heat loss from animals and man. In *Heat loss from animals and man*. Eds. J. L. MONTEITH and L. E. MOUNT, Butterworths, London, pp. 33–58.
COLLINS, K. J. and WEINER, J. S. (1968) Endocrinological aspects of exposure to high environmental temperatures. *Physiol. Rev.*, **48**, 785–839.
FOX, R. H. (1974) Heat acclimatization and the sweating response. In *Heat loss from animals and man*. Eds. J. L. MONTEITH and L. E. MOUNT, Butterworths, London, pp. 277–303.
HALDANE, J. S. (1905) The influence of high air temperatures. *J. Hyg.* (Cambridge), **5**, 494–513.
HATCH, T. F. (1963) Assessment of heat stress. In *Temperature, its Measurement and Control in Science and Industry*. Vol. 3, Pt 3. Eds. C. M. HERTZFIELD and J. D. HARDY. Reinhold, New York, pp. 307–318.
HERTZMAN, A. B. (1959) Vasomotor regulation of cutaneous circulation. *Physiol. Rev.*, **39**, 280–306.
INGRAM, D. L. and MOUNT, L. E. (1975) *Man and Animals in hot environments*. Springer Verlag, New York and Heidelberg, Berlin.
INGRAM, D. L. and MOUNT, L. E. (1976) Solar radiation and heat balance in animals and man. In *Light as an ecological factor II*. Eds. G. C. EVANS, O. RACKHAM and R. BAINBRIDGE, Blackwell, Oxford.
KERSLAKE, D. McE. (1972) *The Stress of Hot Environments*. Cambridge University Press, London.
KUNO, Y. (1956) *The Physiology of Human Perspiration* (2nd ed.). Churchill, London.

LEITHEAD, C. S. and LIND, A. R. (1964) *Heat Stress and Heat Disorders*. Cassell, London.
MONTEITH, J. L. (1973) *Principles of Environmental Physics*. Edward Arnold, London.
SCHMIDT-NIELSEN, K. (1964) *Desert Animals*. Oxford University Press, London.
UNDERWOOD, C. R. and WARD, E. J. (1966) The solar radiation area of man. *Ergonomics*, **9**, 155–168.
WEINER, J. S. and HELLMAN, K. (1960) The sweat glands. *Biol. Rev.*, **35**, 141–186.

THE DEVELOPMENT OF YOUNG
CHILDREN IN A WEST AFRICAN VILLAGE:
A STUDY IN HUMAN ECOLOGY

A. M. THOMSON

MANY international and national agencies are concerned with the health and development of young children in the tropics. Unfortunately, there has been an enormous increase in the number of children, without much improvement, if any, in their general health and well-being. For all its triumphs, preventive medicine has little reason to be pleased with itself in relation to the problems of early life in pre-industrial or developing countries. One of the reasons may be that remarkably few studies have been made of communities at a "grass-roots" level, and even fewer from a comprehensive point of view.

The aim of ecological research is to obtain a synoptic view of the situation as a whole, and the first problem is to know where to start. A multiplicity of phenomena present themselves, to the study of which many different scientific disciplines are relevant. Should one concentrate primarily on food and feeding, or on disease, or on patterns of behaviour? Each facet, taken by itself, could easily come to imply a complex research project, and any attempt to embrace a range of phenomena is apt to be bogged down in a proliferation of detail and a mounting burden of costs and administration.

The question of where to begin loomed large when, a few years ago, we became interested in the health and development of children in Keneba, a small village in the Gambia. Dr. Ian McGregor, Director of the Medical Research Council's laboratories in that country, was first on the scene. His particular interest was tropical medicine, and in order to pursue his investigation, particularly of malaria, he chose Keneba as a suitable locus for studies of a rural community where the traditional subsistence economy, based on agriculture, had prevailed for generations with little modification by the impact of commerce and Western ideas and resources. *Inter alia*, he made a preliminary census of the village and arranged for births and deaths to be recorded locally. Every child was examined annually, in March or April, both as a check on the demographic records and also as a means of obtaining basic data on growth and health. This work started in 1949.

In 1959 I visited the Gambia, and was introduced to the unique set of records that Dr. McGregor had compiled. Out of the annual record cards, we selected those for 187 children born on known dates during the years 1949–53, who had been examined annually until they died or attained the age of seven. The following summarizes the results of an analysis, and the main conclusions reached (McGregor *et al.*, 1961).

Mortality was high. Of the 187 live-born children, 43 % died before reaching the age of seven years. Most of the deaths occurred during the first four years of life, and the death rate reached a peak around one year of age. Two-thirds of the deaths occurred during the rainy months, July to October, when diseases transmitted by insect vectors, notably malaria, reach a peak. The fact that children born in the second half of the year, July to December, were more likely to die when aged 9–14 months than those born during the first half of the year, suggested that an important factor might be the transition between passive and active immunity, and the timing of the first major exposure to infectious diseases.

Growth showed a pattern which has been reported from many tropical countries. During the first few months of life, gains in weight and length were extremely satisfactory by comparison with British and American standards, implying excellent standards of lactation. During the second half of the first year of life and most of the second year, growth faltered markedly. Thereafter, the annual increments were much the same as in Britain, but the leeway was not made up. Thus, the growth curve after about two years of age was parallel to, but well below, that of British children. An interesting feature was that the children who died were practically as big at their last physical examination as children who survived. Thus, any defect of growth which preceded death seemed unlikely to be of long duration.

During the course of their work, Dr. McGregor and his colleagues in the Gambia had become familiar with many aspects of life in the village. A notable feature was that women were entirely responsible for growing, cultivating, and harvesting a main food crop, rice. Work in the rice fields was particularly intense during the rainy season, when old food stocks were running low, and when the transmission of many diseases reached a peak. Pregnancy and lactation did not exonerate women from rice farming, and young babies were usually carried to the fields while their mothers worked. Toddlers were usually left in the care of the old, the unfit, and older children. Mothers were superstitious and were completely ignorant of Western concepts of medicine; indeed, illness was scarcely recognized as calling for action, unless it was obvious and serious. The ailing child with a poor appetite might rapidly become seriously undernourished, because no special action was taken to provide it with suitable food. Putting together the available evidence, we postulated that infectious diseases and unsatisfactory care were the main reasons for high death-rates and for poor growth in these children. Food supplies might be short before the annual harvest, and the feeding of young children might be misguided in practice; but on the whole under-nutrition and malnutrition seemed more often to be secondary to disease than primary.

It was clear that the situation required more intensive investigation.

The Approach to an Intensive Study

On the hypothesis that disease, poor care, and poor feeding were the major causes of high mortality and impaired growth, it seemed to us that a general ecological study should be led by a physician, a sociologist, and a nutritionist, who would work in collaboration to cover these three factors. The study should extend for at least two years, so that changes with season could be adequately covered; during the second year, any mistakes made during the first year might be rectified.

There were immediate difficulties, both in justifying so expensive a project and in finding suitable staff. Eventually we had to scrap the idea of recruiting a physician and a nutritionist; but we were fortunate in interesting a sociologist, Dr. Barbara Thompson, whose outlook was sufficiently flexible to encompass fields of inquiry which were not, strictly, her professional business and who was willing to live in Keneba for two years. She thus became the key figure in the field, and

Dr. McGregor made arrangements to provide part-time medical cover from members of his unit, together with all the necessary logistic support.

We solved the problem of where to begin by building on an intensive study of physical growth. If every child in the village who was aged under five years was weighed at short intervals this would certainly yield a very detailed picture of growth patterns. It would also ensure that every child was seen regularly, and failure to grow in a satisfactory manner would give an early indication of illness or of unsatisfactory feeding.

Children who were obviously ill, or who were failing to gain weight, would be seen by the visiting physician, who made a 100-mile road journey to the village once a week. Several different doctors were involved, and we tried to reduce the amount of "observer variation' by designing forms in which signs and symptoms were recorded in a standardized manner. Disease had to be treated, but it was not easy to decide when powerful modern drugs should be employed. For example, the free use of antimalarial drugs in cases of suspected but unproved malaria would make it extremely difficult to obtain an accurate idea of the true prevalence of malaria. We decided that symptomatic treatment could be given freely, but that specific treatment should be given in cases of serious illness only, and then preferably after a definite diagnosis had been made.

Dr. Thompson, with advice from Professor Raymond Illsley, made plans for sociological and demographic studies. In addition to a vast amount of information collected more or less casually as she moved about the village, a number of specific studies were made. During the first year, three compounds (enclosures inhabited by groups of patrilineally linked families) were visited regularly to record patterns of activity and behaviour, with special reference to child care. During the second year, a small group of young children was observed daily, to obtain more detailed information on who was looking after them, what they were doing, what food was available, and so on.

During the course of the two-year survey (1962–3) care was taken to keep the records up to date, and some of us visited Keneba at intervals to make quick analyses of the available data, to review the course of the work, and to revise plans as necessary. By such means, it was possible to avoid at least some of the mistakes that might have been made, and to seize opportunities that had not been foreseen.

The fact that the periodic reviews were made by a group of specialists representing several scientific disciplines ensured that the overall view remained wide.

Results

Here, it is possible to give only a brief sketch of the results. A general account of the background will be found in a paper by Thomson et al. (1968) and in a thesis by Thompson (1965). Papers have been published on the patterns of growth in relation to age, season, and mortality (McGregor et al., 1968), the early life of infants (Thompson, 1966), infant feeding, and child-care practices (Thompson and Rahman, 1967), the haematological findings (McGregor et al., 1966), aspects of pregnancy and lactation (Thomson et al., 1966; Thompson and Baird, 1967).

Growth

The first thing that became clear was that growth in weight showed marked seasonal variations (Fig. 1). In general, children grew very well during the dry season, November to April, and poorly during the wet season, May to October. The patterns were affected by season of birth. Babies under six months of age grew well even during the

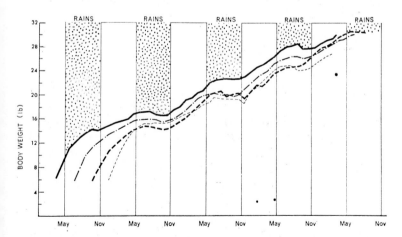

FIG. 1. Average growth curves of four cohorts of children born at different times of year and measured at short intervals during the two years 1962–3.

rainy season: their health was by and large satisfactory, and the presumption is that the immunity which they had acquired passively during intra-uterine life sufficed to protect them against many infections. Their nutritional state was good, and it is interesting that the mothers who were breast-feeding them were able to do so without losing weight, except at the height of the agricultural season when they were unusually active.

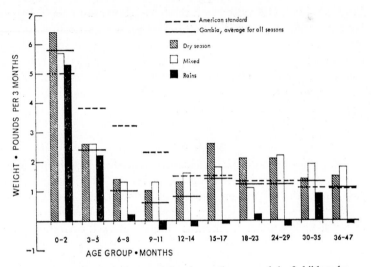

FIG. 2. Average growth rates (pounds per three months) of children by season. The "mixed" groups consist of children for whom the specified age-range covered both the dry and wet season.

Figure 2 gives the weight data in terms of growth velocities. The Boston growth standards (Nelson, 1964) are inserted for purposes of comparison. At all seasons Gambian babies under three months of age grew faster than American babies. During the second half of the first year, the situation had been reversed. Gambian children grew much more slowly than American children, and growth in weight during the rainy season (May to November) was, for all practical purposes, zero. From about 15 months of age, the average annual growth rates were fairly close to those of American children; but the averages conceal a remarkable seasonal variation. During the wet months, growth in weight was zero or slightly negative, but during the dry months there was "catch up", during which growth rates exceeded by a considerable margin those of American children of comparable age. There can be little question that, during the dry months at any rate, the diets of toddlers were sufficient to support very high rates of growth. Trends in height followed patterns fairly similar to those of weight.

Disease

Data on morbidity and mortality have not yet been fully analysed, but preliminary work on them leaves little doubt that disease is the most important cause of faltering growth. This is illustrated by Figs. 3 and 4.

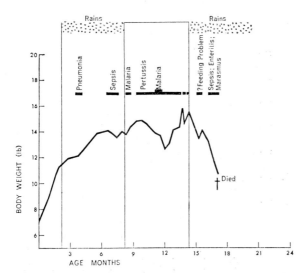

FIG. 3. Growth curve and health of a child who died in a marasmic state
at age 17 months.

Case No. 120 (Fig. 3) died when 17 months of age, and was breast-fed throughout. Growth was satisfactory during the first six months of life, apart from a sharp respiratory infection which responded to penicillin. The first serious setback to growth occurred at about six months of age, near the end of the rains, when she had multiple septic lesions of the skin and showed malaria parasites in the blood. When the rains stopped, growth was again satisfactory for a time,

I

until a further and more serious setback was associated with a persistent episode of whooping cough, during which malaria parasites were again observed. Recovery was halted at the start of the second rainy season in late May, when she was noted to be vaguely ill and to be refusing food other than breast milk. No specific diagnosis was made. She seemed to be recovering during the later part of June, but in July there was a severe episode of diarrhoea and vomiting, together with infection of the middle ear and other septic lesions. The child became severely dehydrated and marasmic, and died when 17 months old. Treatment by the research team was resisted because it was said to be incompatible with native treatment and, finally, because "Allah did not wish the child to grow up and be an adult".

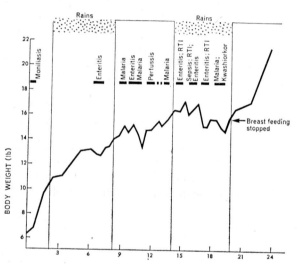

FIG. 4. Growth curve and health of a child who developed signs of kwashiorkor at about 20 months of age.

Case No. 123 (Fig. 4) grew very well until about nine months of age, despite a mild attack of oral thrush shortly after birth, and mild gastroenteritis at about seven months. Malaria, and a further bout of enteritis early in the dry season, failed to cause any serious setback but, as with the previous child, whooping cough caused a considerable loss of weight. The onset of the second rainy season was associated with a succession of intestinal, respiratory, and skin infections, and condition was gradually lost until, near the end of the rains, the clinical diagnosis of kwashiorkor was made. This is a severe malnutritional state, accompanied by oedema, considered to be due to protein deficiency. This particular child had been receiving breast milk throughout, and to my mind the deficiency was secondary to repeated infections rather than the result of a primary dietary defect. The mother was given supplies of dried milk, which were probably fed to the child. Rapid recovery ensued, at the end of the rainy season, without further special treatment.

We hope that the analysis of the morbidity data will give a more systematic picture of the annual cycles of disease and recovery. Malaria, for example, reaches its peak intensity during the second half of the rainy season, and is accompanied by a sharp increase in the amount of anaemia. We do not yet know clearly why growth falters so regularly at the beginning of the rains, in late May or early June. Certainly this is not a function of malaria.

Births and Deaths

There were 68 births in 1962 and 31 in 1963. The former number was nearly twice the expected number, and fortunately an explanation was available. There is a taboo on sexual intercourse during lactation, but conception usually follows soon after the death or weaning of a child. During the spring of 1961, there had been a severe epidemic of measles, which killed many babies and young children (McGregor, 1964). A large number of births followed about a year later.

There were ten deaths in 1962 and 25 in 1963. The larger number during the second year was, of course, due to the influx of an unusually large number of children at the most vulnerable age— around one year. It would appear that, although nearly every child was treated at least once with a powerful drug, and about 5% were admitted to hospital, we made rather little impression on the flood of disease.

In conformity with the findings in the preliminary study, the age-specific weights of children who died were little different from those of survivors. There were 23 deaths where measurements of growth had been made for at least two "quarters" (i.e. half the dry or the rainy season) preceding death. The behaviour of weight appears to depend to some extent on the season at which death occurs. To summarize, deaths during the rainy season appeared to be the result of acute illness, often accompanied by a rapid loss of weight of short duration. Deaths during the dry season occurred more often in children whose growth had been faltering for a relatively long period, so that they were underweight when the terminal illness supervened. It proved to be exceedingly difficult to arrive at any clear-cut conclusions on causes of death. The causes were almost invariably multiple, and to list the nature of the terminal illness only would give a misleading picture.

Many of these very ill children presented all the characteristics of severe malnutrition and undernutrition: they could, indeed, have been used very well to illustrate the posters of agencies devoted to the relief of hunger. But there is no reason to believe that flooding the village with extra food would have done much good. Indeed, the free issue of dried milk might easily have caused more deaths than it prevented. One has only to observe the unhygienic conditions under which such milk is prepared and fed to babies to realize how it can cause gastroenteritis. In another Gambian village, the dried milk provided by an international agency was known locally as "the stuff that causes diarrhoea".

I have already said that most mothers were able to lactate abundantly—another fact which probably argues against general shortage of food. It is of interest that babies were commonly fed from the breast not only by the mother, but also by other female relatives who were lactating. The care of babies whose mothers were ill or who died was taken over by others, often very effectively. There is a Gambian saying: "fat as an orphan baby".

Attitudes to Western Medicine

Throughout the period during which research had been undertaken in the village, scientific staff treated villagers who came for help. On the other hand, treatment was rarely pressed upon villagers, and no medical "propaganda" was undertaken. The research workers could not afford to provide a continuous medical service on which the villagers might become dependent, and which the government of the country could not afford to take over. Thus, the situation arose that the community had continuous access to its indigenous resources and also, intermittently, to the resources of Western medicine.

Attitudes were curiously ambivalent. On the one hand, it was agreed that the Western doctors could sometimes produce miraculous cures. On the other hand, the general superiority of Western medicine was by no means universally accepted, and its concepts were probably not understood at all. Most illness was thought to be of mystical origin. For example, a bad "Satan" was thought to be responsible for most serious or recurrent illnesses, and a specific ethnic influence had to be identified to effect a cure, for which European medicine was frequently considered to be useless. Logic was not absent from such concepts. For example, delirium was thought to indicate that the Devil was inside the patient; and as Allah had been cheated by the Devil, it was reasonable to be frightened of the patient, and recovery might be undesirable. It was reported, apparently with some justification, that the survivors of delirium were often mentally abnormal and unable to fulfil their role in society. Thus, instead of taking curative action, it was considered appropriate to take measures which would ease the sufferers' passage to Paradise. Ideas such as these, together with a deep-seated belief in the efficacy of traditional remedies, explained why the assistance of the research team was often invoked as a last resort, when it might be too late to give effective treatment, and why patients under treatment were sometimes withdrawn. There were occasions when the research staff, unable to help, had reason to be thankful for the villagers' quiet acceptance of "the will of Allah".

It is doubtful whether these villagers felt deprived because no continuous medical service of Western type was available. Their traditional resources and remedies had served them well for generations. Western medicine was definitely "on trial", and perhaps the fact that it was available without fee caused it to be viewed with some misgiving as a not-necessarily benevolent agency of the Government.

Medical treatment thus had many difficulties to overcome. Preventive medicine was even less straightforward, since it implied radical changes in attitudes and customs. In local eyes, this was mainly a matter of charms and rituals. Traditional habits die hard. I have watched the destruction of a concrete latrine erected by the Government as a measure against the spread of hookworm. It had never been much used, the people preferring to go into the fields as usual, and the fragments made excellent building material. In the Gambia, and many other areas of West Africa, the prevention of malaria by eradicating anopheline mosquitoes is impossibly difficult and expensive, and local control of insects, for example by spraying the huts with insecticides, is relatively ineffectual. The issue of malaria suppressive drugs, requiring strict discipline and regularity in use, would also be of little value in such a community. Furthermore, such drugs might simply postpone the age at which immunity is acquired by exposure to the disease. Older Gambian children, and Gambian adults, have a remarkably high level of immunity to malaria, which causes little more upset than the common cold in this country.

I have little doubt that the provision of a permanent medical centre in the village, adequately stocked by modern drugs and staffed by enthusiasts, could transform the health situation in Keneba. But this is no model for the health service of an impoverished country with hundreds of rural communities in it.

I suspect that the provision of a supply of pure tap-water might be a potent force for good, as it was in Britain during the nineteenth century. At present, the mothers of Keneba draw turbid and probably contaminated water by hand from wells about 18 m deep. Plentiful, clean water would not only improve environmental hygiene, but taps would also save time, especially during the busy season. Modern immunization procedures would almost certainly be worthwhile, since they are relatively cheap, and require little co-operation on the part of the populace. Injections are readily accepted, because the native practitioners of "bush medicine" have no equivalent.

CARE OF YOUNG CHILDREN

Children are prized, and are not neglected. But the care they receive is unsatisfactory in many ways, because of the unhygienic environment, ignorance of the principles of preventive and curative medicine and the burden of agricultural work which falls on the women. The women *must* work in the rice fields to provide sufficient food. I am not competent to discuss the organization of labour and its productivity. Haswell (1963) had given a detailed account of another Gambian village, and comments that women "will inevitably continue to play a major role in agricultural production as long as there is no significant improvement in the level of living which, in 1949, was little more than bare subsistence". Mothers busy in the fields have no choice but to leave children in the care of those who are too old or infirm, or are too young, to work. Naturally, the toddler, who is not yet old enough to fend for himself, is the sufferer. It is of interest that the economic status of the family groups in Keneba appeared to have little influence upon the health of the child. "Wealth" meant cattle, a tin roof instead of thatch on the roof, it made little or no difference to the immediate environment of the child or to the way in which it was handled.

I have wondered whether it would be possible to persuade the villagers to organize a "day nursery" where dependent children could be looked after, perhaps, by one trained person with unskilled assistance. Such a nursery could form a focus for education and immunization and for the early diagnosis of illness, quite apart from its main function, that of ensuring the adequate supervision and feeding of children while their mothers were at work. Yet Dr. McGregor, who knows the village much better than I do, points out that such a scheme would be almost bound to fail unless it were promoted by the villagers themselves. It implies a break with tradition and, without spontaneous (even if "engineered") local support, would have limited effect. Furthermore, any disaster, such as the death of a child while in the nursery, could easily be interpreted as a sign that the will of Allah was being flouted.

I have indicated that the nutritional situation seems to be not unsatisfactory, in so far as food supplies are concerned. This is true except for two or three months before the autumn harvest, when food stocks may be very low. Adults certainly lose weight from late July to early October, both because food is relatively scarce, and because very hard work is being undertaken in the fields (Thomson *et al.*, 1966). At the same time, the variety of foods available for young children is reduced, and the mothers are too busy to ensure that what is available for young children is actually eaten. This is the season, too, when the onslaught of diseases reaches its peak, and when the climate is most trying. Loss of appetite may easily turn a minor illness into a serious one. The problem is by no means simply one of providing more food suitable for consumption by young children.

General Conclusions

In a situation such as I have described, there are no simple remedies for high mortality and morbidity rates, and for impaired growth among young children. There is no doubt that the applications of modern techniques of preventive and curative medicine could transform the situation, but the provision of such techniques is beyond the means of a poor country and their acceptance by the population would require an economic and educational revolution, implying transformation of the whole way of life.

In populations living in and around the larger towns this transformation is occurring as a result of new economic and political forces. The process would be less erratic and wasteful if the facts were carefully established by systematic ecological research.

It might be objected that the ultimate consequences would be disastrous because lower death rates would mean a rapidly increasing population. There is perhaps some comfort in Haswell's (1963) view that: "Growth of population is indispensable to any significant improvement in the general economic level—and incomes in Africa are among the lowest in the world".

Acknowlegements

I am solely responsible for this account of investigations which were undertaken by a team; but I wish to thank my colleagues, most of whom are mentioned by name in the text or in the references, for collecting the facts and for debating them with me.

The final report was published in 1970 (McGregor, I. A., Rahman, A. K., Thomson, A. M., Billewicz, W. Z. and Thompson, B., *Trans. Roy. Soc. Trop. Med. Hyg.*, **64,** 48).

References

HASWELL, M. R. (1963) *The Changing Pattern of Economic Activity in a Gambian Village*, Dept. Techn. Coop. Overseas Research Publ. No. 2. H.M.S.O. London.

McGREGOR, I. A., RAHMAN, A. K., THOMPSON, B., BILLEWICZ, W. Z. and THOMSON, A. M. (1968) *Trans. Roy. Soc. Trop. Med. Hyg.*, **62,** 341.

McGREGOR, I. A. (1964) *W. Afr. Med. J.*, **13,** 251.

McGREGOR, I. A., BILLEWICZ, W. Z. and THOMSON, A. M. (1961) *Brit. Med. J.*, ii. 1661.

McGREGOR, I. A., WILLIAMS, K., BILLEWICZ, W. Z. and THOMSON, A. M. (1966) *Trans. Roy. Soc. Trop. Med. Hyg.*, **60,** 650.

NELSON, W. E. (1964) *Textbook of Pediatrics*, 8th Ed. W. B. Saunders Company, Philadelphia and London.

THOMPSON, B. (1965) *Marriage, Childbirth and Early Childhood in a Gambian Village: a Socio-medical Study*. Thesis, University of Aberdeen.

THOMPSON, B. (1966) *Lancet*, ii. 40.

THOMPSON, B. and BAIRD, D. (1967) *J. Obstet. Gynaec. Brit. Commonw.*, **74,** 329, 499 and 510.

THOMPSON, B. and RAHMAN, A. K. (1967) *J. Trop. Pediat.*, **13,** 124.

THOMSON, A. M., BILLEWICZ, W. Z., THOMPSON, B. and McGREGOR, I. A. (1966) *J. Obstet, Gynaec. Brit. Commonw.*, **73,** 724.

THOMSON, A. M., BILLEWICZ, W. Z., THOMPSON, B., ILLSLEY, R., RAHMAN, A. K. and McGREGOR, I. A. (1968) *Trans. Roy. Soc. Trop. Med. Hyg.*, **62,** 330.

THE ECOLOGY OF
AFRICAN SCHISTOSOMIASIS

C. A. WRIGHT

THE disease known as schistosomiasis or bilharziasis is caused by parasitic flatworms of the family Schistosomatidae. The adult flukes live in the venous system of warm-blooded animals and the larval stages develop in freshwater snails. The life-cycle is very direct; eggs laid by the adult parasites work their way through the wall of the blood vessel in which the adults live, then through the tissues of the host's intestine or bladder and are eventually voided in the faeces or urine of the host. If the eggs fall into freshwater they hatch and a ciliated larva (miracidium) emerges. Miracidia swim freely in water but have a brief life-expectancy and they must find and enter a suitable snail host within a few hours. Inside the snail the larva undergoes metamorphosis to a mother sporocyst, a simple, sac-like organism within the lumen of which a number of daughter sporocysts are produced. These daughter sporocysts leave the mother and migrate to the digestive gland of the snail where they settle and grow. Within each daughter are formed large numbers of the final larval stage, the cercaria, which is simply a juvenile fluke equipped with a large forked tail. When mature (about four weeks after initial penetration of the snail by the miracidium) the cercariae leave the snail and swim free in the water, their free active life is no longer than that of the miracidia and they must enter their final host within a few hours of emerging from the snail. Entry is effected by direct penetration of the host's skin and any form of contact with water containing cercariae therefore places the host at risk of infection. During penetration the forked tail is cast off and once within the sub-dermal layers of the host the larva (which is now called a schistosomula) enters the lymphatic system and thence the blood vessels. After various migrations during which the young worms mature they become established in their habitat of choice, usually some part of the portal venous system, and commence egg-laying.

The principal species of schistosome parasitic in man are *Schistosoma japonicum* in the Far East and *S. haematobium* and *S. mansoni* in Africa and adjacent areas. A third species in Africa, *S. intercalatum*, although somewhat restricted in its range, is worthy of inclusion because of the contrasts which it shows to the other two African species. The family Schistosomatidae has a more or less world-wide distribution and its members parasitize a wide range of birds and mammals but it is the African parasites of man with which we are concerned here. *S. haematobium* is normally parasitic in the veins of the pelvic plexus, particularly those of the bladder wall, and the eggs are voided in the host's urine. The snail hosts for this parasite are species of the planorbid genus *Bulinus*, a characteristic element of the Ethiopian freshwater fauna, whose range extends into southern Europe, the Middle East and some of the islands surrounding Africa. *S. mansoni* adults live in the mesenteric veins of man and their eggs are passed out in the faeces. Planorbid snails (belonging to the genus *Biomphalaria*) serve as hosts for *S. mansoni*. *Biomphalaria* has a more restricted Ethiopian range than *Bulinus* but also occurs in the Neotropical region thus enabling *S. mansoni* to become established in parts of South America and the Caribbean area. *S. intercalatum*, although closely related to *S. haematobium*, is, like *S. mansoni*, a parasite of the mesenteric veins. The snail hosts of *S. intercalatum* are members of the genus *Bulinus* but the parasite is known only from some parts of the Congo Basin and the Lower Guinea rain forest area.

The adults of *S. mansoni* and *S. haematobium* are very specific to man and despite occasional records of *S. mansoni* in other mammals, it is doubtful whether either species can exist in the absence of man. *S. intercalatum* on the other hand is, under experimental conditions, capable of developing successfully in a wider range of hosts and there is reason to believe that this species may be originally a parasite of forest-living monkeys to which man becomes exposed when he intrudes into the transmission area (Wright *et al.*, 1972).

The larval stages of all three species are very exacting in the specificity of their snail host requirements and this is particularly true of *S. haematobium* and *S. intercalatum*. Although this volume is concerned mainly with human ecology it is necessary to stress that an exaggerated anthropocentric approach to schistomiasis throws too much emphasis on one phase of the life-cycle. The parasites are the only direct connection between man and the snails concerned and the real centre of attention must be the ecology of the life-cycle as a whole. Schistosomes, and therefore schistosomiasis, can only exist in an active state where the ecology of man brings him into physical contact with appropriate snail habitats. An important ecological distinction between schistosomiasis and insect-borne diseases must also be understood. In the transmission of a parasite by blood-feeding insects as, for instance, malaria, the mosquitoes or other flies are vectors, active distributive agents carrying the parasite from person to person, but in schistosomiasis the snail is *not* a vector, it is a passive intermediate host which plays no active part in distribution of the disease (Wright, 1960). Although actual penetration of the snail is achieved by the free-swimming miracidium the distributive agent responsible for transporting the disease from one snail habitat to another is man. A further distinction between insect-borne diseases and schistosomiasis is that there is no need for any physical contact between the two hosts in the cycle, thus the behaviour patterns of the two free-swimming larval stages are of as much importance to successful transmission as is the behaviour of the molluscan and vertebrate hosts.

Origins of Schistosome Host-parasite Relationships

Before considering the contemporary distribution and transmission of the schistosomes parasitic in man in Africa it is worth making a few speculations about their evolutionary origins. Palaeontological evidence shows that at least one of the present-day species groups of *Bulinus* was clearly differentiated in early Pleistocene times (Leriche, 1925). The presence of a somewhat generalized "relic" species belonging to the same complex (*B. obtusispira*) on Madagascar points to the divergence of that group (*B. africanus* group) prior to the separation of Madagascar from continental Africa (Wright, 1971) and it is probable that, despite the paucity of the fossil record, both bulinid and biomphalaria snails have been an important element of the African freshwater fauna for a long time. During the Miocene in East Africa there was a phase of explosive evolution of primates which eventually led to the appearance of early hominids between 3 and 4 million years ago. At that time schistosomes parasitic in other mammals almost certainly already existed and the rapidly evolving primates, particularly those whose habits brought them into frequent close contact with water, would have provided excellent potential hosts.

The total fossil assemblages found together with early hominid remains indicate that the fauna was of a savanna type, possibly with some gallery forest influences (Leakey, 1973) and some of the later sites appear to have been closely associated with water, especially shallow lake margins (Cole, 1964). It has been suggested that in such situations early man would have been able to prey upon other animals drinking at the water's edge by driving them into the lake and killing them with stones. In time the more settled communities of the Mesolithic cultures appeared, often with an economy based at least in part on fishing and the close association with water was retained. Throughout this period climate played an important role in determining the areas suitable for human habitation and no prehistoric remains have been found in East Africa above an altitude of 1800 m (Cole, 1964). The climate under such conditions would have been ideal for completion of the schistosome life-cycle and even today there is little or no transmission above 1800 m largely because above this altitude water temperatures tend to be too low for satisfactory development of the larval stages in snails. Pastoral and agricultural communities which developed later were still dependent upon water and the connection between man and snail habitats was thus continued. Not only was East Africa one of the centres of man's evolutionary origin but it was also probably the origin of the bulinid hosts for *S. haematobium* (Wright, 1961). Thus, throughout the early stages of human evolution both of the hosts necessary to the schistosome life-cycle were continually in close contact under conditions ideally suited to transmission of the parasites. In these circumstances it was possible for the very specific host-parasite relationships of *S. haematobium* and *S. mansoni* to evolve.

The situation with respect to *S. intercalatum* appears to be quite different. As has already been mentioned this parasite is known only from the forest areas of Lower Guinea and the Congo basin and in these two general foci the snail hosts for the parasite are different (and mutually incompatible). This suggests that the two centres of transmission have been isolated from one another for a considerable period. Although snails potentially susceptible to both strains of *S. intercalatum* exist all through the savanna regions this parasite appears never to have established itself outside the forest areas. A possible explanation for this lies in the thermal tolerance of the cercariae which is lower than that of the savanna species (Southgate, in preparation) and this, together with the peculiar habit of this larval stage of *S. intercalatum* of concentrating immediately beneath the surface film, may prevent the species from extending into areas where full sun exposure raises the surface layer of the water to temperatures beyond the tolerance limits of the cercariae. The evidence discussed by Wright *et al.* (1972) pointed fairly strongly towards *S. intercalatum* being originally a parasite of forest-dwelling monkeys (possibly *Cercocebus* or *Cercopithecus* spp.) to which man becomes exposed as a result of forest clearing and other activities. Some support for this idea has recently been forthcoming from Dr. H. B. van Wijk (private communication) who encountered a number of cases of infection with *S. intercalatum* among people in the recently cleared area of new Deido on the edge of Douala, Cameroon, where the parasite had not previously been recorded.

Historical Evidence of Schistosomiasis

One of the earliest known permanent communities, the Neolithic city of Jericho, depended on the presence of a prolific spring which created an oasis in an otherwise inhospitable desert area. On the basis of a single juvenile shell of *Bulinus truncatus* found inside another freshwater shell embedded in mud used for building in later (Bronze Age) Jericho, Biggs (1960) has suggested that the inhabitants may have suffered from schistosomiasis. He has developed this hypothesis further with the conjecture that as a result of the debilitating effects of the disease the people of Jericho may have become listless and inattentive to the repair of the city walls. Thus, when Joshua and his army attacked, the "more virile and parasite-free desert dwellers were more than a match for the inhabitants". Girges (1934) quotes more tangible evidence for the existence of schistosomiasis in early Egypt from the mention of haematuria (the most obvious but not necessarily diagnostic symptom of *S. haematobium* infection) in the Kahun papyrus of the twelfth or thirteenth dynasty (about 2000 B.C.). The Ebers papyrus of about 1500 B.C. contains methods for the treatment of haematuria, and Girges suggests that the penis-shields portrayed on the walls of some early Egyptian temples might have been a prophylactic device against the disease. However, the earliest definite evidence of human schistosomiasis was provided by Ruffer's (1910) demonstration of the parasite eggs in tissues of Egyptian mummies of the twentieth dynasty (about 1250–1000 B.C.). It was this observation, together with the known prevalence of the disease in modern Egypt, which has led to the belief that schistosomiasis had a Nilotic origin, but, as I have tried to show, the real origins of the disease probably lie further to the south and a great deal earlier in time.

About one-third of the African continent is subject to hot, over-watered conditions and about a quarter of the land surface suffers from severe water shortages (Last, 1965). The distribution of the human population is affected by the rainfall pattern and tends to be concentrated where conditions are most favourable for agriculture. About 20% of the inhabitants live in arid or very arid areas where the rainfall is less than 250 mm per year; about 22% are in the semi-arid regions where precipitation amounts vary from 250 to 500 mm; 42% live where the rainfall is between 500 to 1500 mm; and only 16% in the excessively wet areas where rainfall exceeds 1500 mm annually (Dekker, 1965). Rainfall figures alone do not give an adequate picture of the surface-water situation, because topography and soil structure affect the run-off, and evaporation rates and seasonal distribution of precipitation influence the permanence of static water bodies.

The situation is further complicated by longer-term climatic changes such as the Sahel drought of the early 1970s. There is evidence from the study of fossil soils in West Africa that during the last 20 000 years there have been considerable shifts in the distribution of the forested areas, reflecting major climatic changes which in turn have influenced the distribution of both human communities and freshwater snails. Obviously freshwater snails will only live where suitable habitats occur but the presence of water is no criterion of suitability. In general the planorbid hosts for schistosomes are not found in heavily shaded situations nor where the water is fast-flowing. As a result the third of Africa that is over-watered is largely free from schistosomiasis because in these areas stream flow tends to be rapid and fringing vegetation provides dense shade. The foci of *S. intercalatum* transmission are exceptions to this general principle and in areas where forest clearing has been followed by established commercial agriculture the other species of schistosomes have extended their range.

In the savanna and semi-arid areas, where the majority of the rural population is concentrated, are the ideal habitats for snail development. In these regions the rainfall tends to be seasonal and there are associated fluctuations in snail population densities. The arid deserts of Africa are not entirely devoid of surface water. Many of the oases which owe their existence to underground sources derived from rainfall on distant mountains provide excellent snail habitats and irrigation schemes are now augmenting and extending these formerly limited foci. Thus, fortunately for the schistosomes, there are similarities in the ecological requirements of both men and snails. Over 60% of the human population is distributed in the savanna areas where the snails are common in a wide variety of habitats, and the majority of the 20% of the population who live in the desert regions are localized in the neighbourhood of oases where man-snail contacts are particularly concentrated.

Although planorbid snails are not markedly active animals, their capacity for passive dispersal is very great. One of their main assets in this respect is that they are potentially self-fertilizing hermaphro-dites and the accidental transport of a single individual to a previously uncolonized habitat is enough to start a new population. In the savanna areas movements of wallowing game animals such as buffalo probably served in the past as the principal distributive agents. In the deserts the movements of nomadic tribes have always been closely linked with available water sources, and a snail accidentally taken up in a water-carrier at one oasis could easily be rinsed out and released at the next. Modern developments such as the creation of earth dams for water conservation, fishponds, and irrigation schemes, are providing further habitats which become populated by snails with great rapidity. In most of these situations it is probably a human agency which is either directly or indirectly responsible for introducing the snails, but the classical vehicle of wading birds' feet cannot be entirely dismissed.

So far as is known, all African species of *Biomphalaria* are in some degree susceptible to infections with *S. mansoni* and, with the notable exception of Angola, this parasite occurs wherever biomphalariid snails are found, provided that climatic conditions are suitable for development of the larval stages. No satisfactory explanation is available for the absence of *S. mansoni* from Angola where *Biomphalaria* is widely distributed throughout the plateau region. The relationship between *S. haematobium* and *S. intercalatum* and the bulinid snails is more complex.

Of the five species groups into which *Bulinus* is divided members of four act as hosts for *S. haematobium* and three for *S. intercalatum*. The fifth—the *B. tropicus* group does not carry either parasite. The *B. truncatus* complex extends throughout the Mediterranean region and the Middle East and occurs in West Africa as far south as Angola. In East Africa there are members of the complex in the Great Lakes and in some of the mountainous regions and they have recently been identified in a variety of habitats in the Kano Plain region and south almost to the Tanzanian border in Kenya (Brown and Wright, 1974; Southgate and Knowles in press).

So far snails of this group have been found to transmit *S. haematobium* only in North and West Africa and the Middle East although laboratory experiments have shown that Kenya populations are susceptible to the parasite and they also serve as natural hosts for *S. bovis*, a parasite of cattle, in Kenya. *B. truncatus* group snails do not carry *S. intercalatum*. The *B. africanus* group occurs only in Africa south of the Sahara with the somewhat aberrant *B. obtusispira* on Madagascar. The members of this group are the principal hosts for *S. haematobium* in Central and Southern Africa and they also act as hosts for *S. intercalatum* in the Congo forest area. The *B. forskali* complex is almost pan-African, extending from the Nile delta to Cape Province and from Senegambia to Somalia. It also occurs in south-west Arabia and on the Indian Ocean islands of Madagascar, Mauritius and Aldabra and has been recorded from the Cape Verde Islands off the north-west coast of Africa. Despite this extensive distribution, members of the *B. forskali* group have only been confirmed as hosts for *S. haematobium* in Mauritius,

Madagascar, south Arabia and the Senegambian region of West Africa. The species of snails involved in these areas appear to be closely related and may have been forced into a pattern of peripheral isolation by parasite pressure (Wright, 1971). *S. intercalatum* in the Lower Guinea region is transmitted by the nominate species of the group (*B. forskali*) which does not normally carry *S. haematobium*. Under experimental conditions all members of the *B. forskali* complex have proved to be susceptible to *S. intercalatum*. The *B. reticulatus* group consists at present of two species only, *B. reticulatus* which occurs in scattered localities, usually in temporary habitats, in east and central southern Africa and *B. wrighti* known only from Arabia. The host role of *B. reticulatus* has not been demonstrated in nature but *B. wrighti* carries *S. haematobium* in south Arabia and in laboratory experiments has proved to be susceptible to all species of *Schistosoma* with terminal spines on their eggs.

The parasites transmitted by the different snail groups are very specific in their intermediate host requirements, and will not normally develop in snails of one of the other groups (Wright, 1966). Within the groups there are further strain differences which manifest themselves by their differential infectivity to other populations of snails of the same group and in differences in their pathological effects on their final hosts. The distribution of the parasites borne by the *forskali* group is particularly interesting, and it is possible that the occurrence of these parasites in West Africa, far removed from other foci of a similar type, is directly due to human activity. There is an extremely strong Muslim influence in West Africa, and as long ago as the fourteenth century Ibn Batuta recorded that pilgrims from this region often made the Haj to Mecca. Many of the pilgrims camp in the Wadi Fatima near Jedda and there is known to be a focus of *forskali* group transmitted schistosomiasis in that place (Azim and Gisman, 1956). This strain of parasite is almost certainly the same as that in south Arabia (Wright, 1963) to which the West African *B. senegalensis* has been shown to be susceptible (Wright, 1962). The longevity of adult schistosomes in man is such that an infection acquired in Arabia could remain active for many years and hence become established in any area visited by the carrier where suitable snails occur.

K

Transmission

The basic requirement for schistosome transmission—contact between man and suitable snail habitats—has already been made clear. However, there are behavioural characteristics of both the parasites and of the human hosts which influence the success of the cycle and which give to each focus of infection its own peculiar nature. For instance, in most areas the greatest concentration of snails within a habitat is usually near to the surface, and the initial responses of miracidia on emergence from their eggs are negatively geotactic and positively phototactic. These responses lead the larvae toward the upper layers of the water where their chances of encountering a suitable host are considerably enhanced (Wright, 1960). However, in an area where the snails are known to live mainly on the bottom, the usual responses were not observed in miracidia of the local strain of parasite and they remained steadily near to the bottom of the container in which they were hatched (Wright, 1962). This observation of apparent positive geotaxis by local populations of *S. haematobium* miracidia in Iraq, confirmed by Wajdi (1972) and Shiff's (1969) experiments in open ponds in Rhodesia, lent weight to the idea that in this parasite species negative phototaxis as well is more frequent than was previously believed. More recently Shiff (1974) has found that in a natural habitat in Rhodesia there is a difference in the phototactic response of the miracidia according to the season of the year. In the winter when the thermal gradient of the water bodies is more marked by accumulation of cooler water near the bottom the greatest number of successful snail infections occurs near to the surface but in the summer when temperatures are uniformly higher throughout the habitat the majority of infections occur on the bottom. Similar temperature-dependent light responses have been recorded for *Schistosoma japonicum* and in both cases the miracidial responses correspond with behaviour changes in the snail hosts. There are also diurnal rhythms in the shedding of cercariae from infected snails, and the peaks in these rhythms tend to coincide with periods of activity of the final hosts. The principal definitive hosts for *S. japonicum* in the Philippine Islands are rats, which are largely nocturnal in their habits, and the peak of cercarial shedding in this species occurs between 1700 and 2000 hours (Pesigan *et al.*, 1958). In East Africa the cercariae of *S. rodhaini*, a parasite of rodents, are shed early in the morning (Fripp, 1963), while the peak production period for the larvae of the two African human parasites is around midday. Another diurnal rhythm which reaches a peak at a time most favourable for transmission of the parasite is seen in the excretion of eggs of *S. haematobium*. This peak occurs around midday or the early afternoon when contact with water is likely to be at its maximum. It was thought at one time that this apparent rhythm was the result of stimulated bladder movements due to physical activity during the early part of the day which released trapped eggs, but it has recently been shown to occur even in patients confined to bed (Jordan, 1963) and therefore appears to be a true endogenous rhythm of the parasite.

Superimposed on these short-term rhythms are the longer seasonal fluctuations due to climatic conditions. I am indebted to Dr. V. de V. Clarke for the following summary of the transmission pattern on the Rhodesian highveldt, which illustrates superbly well the interaction of some of these factors.

In January and February the heavy rains fall. Water levels in static water bodies are high, rivers and streams are in flood, water temperatures are less than the optimum for snail breeding, and many snail populations are severely reduced by the floods. There is only moderate human contact with the water and schistosome transmission is low. During March, April, and May the rains are largely over, the water levels have settled, and temperatures are high enough to maintain snail breeding and sporocyst development. The days are warm and sunny and the people, particularly the children, are liable to have some contact with water. As a result there is an increase in transmission. The winter months of June, July, August, and possibly September are characterized by sunny days but very cold nights, and water temperatures remain low. There is very little snail breeding and the people have as little contact with water as possible. There is also plenty of tall vegetation so that it is not necessary to seek the cover of small depressions such as stream valleys for urination and defecation. During this period there is virtually no transmission. October, November, and December are the very hot months relieved only by occasional thunderstorms in late November and December. Water levels have receded after the winter drought and not only are the snail populations more concentrated but the high temperatures are ideal for rapid breeding and for sporocyst development. The great heat makes water inviting to the people and they tend to have prolonged contact, often entirely immersed, particularly during the middle of the day when cercarial emission from the snails is greatest (and egg-output of *S. haematobium* is at its maximum). The vegetation has become sparse and people seek small topographical depressions to provide cover for defecation and hence tend to pollute the water more frequently. This, then, is the season for maximum schistosome transmission on the highveldt, but in the lowveldt the perennially high water temperatures maintain transmission throughout the year.

Even in areas over which the climatic periodicity is relatively uniform there may be quite different transmission patterns in different communities whose spatial isolation is not great. Such variations are often due to differences in the basic economies of the communities and hence their choice of different sites for villages. These differences in basic economies are often due to tribal differences, and the transmission pattern may be modified by local social or religious practices. A situation of this type which is not yet fully investigated exists in the Gambia, where the area of schistosome transmission is so limited that gross climatic factors are of no account. There are three main tribal groups involved in the area—Mandingo, Fula, and Serahuli. The first tend to live principally in the river valley, where rice-farming is the basis for their economy. The second group are mostly pastoral, herding cattle and growing millet and groundnuts on the low plateau on either side of the river; the third group live in villages near to streams flowing into the main river, and they subsist on mixed farming, some fishing, and trade.

Of the Gambian species of snail which are capable of transmitting schistosomiasis, none live in the main river and they are virtually absent from the rice fields on the flood-plain. Thus there is scarcely any transmission in the river valley itself. On the laterite plateau there are depressions which fill with water during the wet season, and these are the exclusive habitat of *B. senegalensis*, a species of snail capable of withstanding prolonged dry-season desiccation and an excellent host for both *S. haematobium* and the cattle parasite *S. bovis*. These pools, during their seasonal existence, are the centres to which the people come to wash clothes and bathe and at which the cattle are watered. During this time schisosome transmission is intense, but during the dry season it is non-existent. The tributary streams to the main river become turbulent and flooded during the wet season and their snail populations (mostly *Bulinus jousseaumei* and *Biomphalaria pfeifferi*) are severely reduced. After the rains the stream-levels fall rapidly and the residual snail populations breed quickly, so that by the time the streams have become slow-moving and confined within their well-defined banks there are prolific colonies of intermediate hosts available. The edges of these streams are often fringed with fairly dense bush, and consequently human contacts tend to be concentrated at the open places near to bridges and fords where patches of slack water particularly favourable to snail breeding often occur. In these foci the peak of transmission is achieved during the dry season. Thus, within a radius of about 20 miles, it is possible to find communities virtually free from schisto-somiasis, others with high infection rates depending upon wet-season transmission by snails of the *Bulinus forskali* group, and still others with moderate infection rates derived from dry-season trans-mission by snails of the *B. africanus* group. Within this small area there are also a few foci where transmission is probably mostly in the dry season through snails of the *B. truncatus* complex, but at present too little is known about these for useful comments to be made.

The influence of social customs on schistosome transmission is most easily seen in the preference shown by women in rural villages for performing their routine tasks in traditional ways. The daily gathering on the stream bank to wash clothes is an essential part of the social activity of the village. Young children accompany their mothers to the stream and play in the water almost as soon as they can walk and so become exposed to infection at a very early age. The chances of transmission are often improved by the fact that the women will choose for preference a point on a bend in a stream where they can work more closely together, and it is at just such points that eddies and slack water occur which favour snail-breeding sites. Attempts have been made from time to time to provide alternative safe washing facilities in villages where this activity is an important source of transmission, but these alternatives are rarely accepted. It has been suggested that unwillingness to utilize these facilities is symptomatic of the inherent resistance to change which is often encountered even in more sophisiticated communities, but there appears to have been little hesitation in the adoption of modern soaps and detergents. It seems more likely that in designing such washing places inadequate attention has been given to either their physical nature, which may entail an unaccustomed posture for this type of work, or to the psychological importance of the daily gathering of women away from the immediate surroundings of the village.

An even greater problem among Muslim peoples in schistosome endemic areas are the ritual ablutions before prayer and the custom of washing the anus with water after defecation. The second of these activities leads to the use of stream banks (and similar places where water is readily available) as latrines, and hence automatically increases the risk of direct pollution. However, direct faecal contamination of the water is not necessary for transmission, because the eggs of *S. mansoni* often adhere to the perianal region and they can subsequently be washed off and hatch successfully. In the Yemen the ablution basins of the mosques are often infested with *Biomphalaria* snails and are some of the most important sites for the transmission of *S. mansoni* (Kuntz, 1952).

These are only two aspects of human behaviour which can influence greatly the patterns of transmission in particular areas. Unfortunately the early stages of schistosomiasis research were hampered by a misinterpretation of the vector role of the snails, a misguided but understandable extrapolation from the more advanced studies on insect-borne diseases. As a result the emphasis of ecological work was placed on molluscan hosts and too little attention was given to the infinitely complex question of human behaviour. It is to be hoped that more effort will be directed towards this problem in the future and there is no doubt that the data gained will be of the greatest value in effective control measures.

Prospects of Control

A few general observations on the prospects of schistosomiasis control may make an appropriate conclusion to this broad outline of the ecology of the disease, for it is only on a sound knowledge of the ecological factors involved in its transmission that effective control can be based. The obvious objective must be the elimination of contacts between infected people and potential transmission sites inhabited by snails. So far the most favoured approach has been based on destruction of the snails with molluscicidal chemicals.

Early attempts in this direction were clumsy and unsuccessful, the chemicals often doing more damage to other elements of the fauna than to the snails. In recent years more specific compounds with greater toxicity have been produced, and in certain situations, such as irrigation systems and well-defined agricultural areas, a considerable measure of success has been gained, but always at the price of constant vigilance, for a single survivor from a treatment is enough to start a new colony.

The other obvious point of attack in the cycle—elimination of the adult worms in infected people—suffered the same early failures. Until recently the drugs available for treatment of schistosomiasis were not as effective as might be desired and required prolonged courses of administration; the majority of them also had unpleasant side-effects which made people unwilling to complete the necessary course. Although successful cures were often obtained with these drugs when used on individual cases under proper supervision, they were of little value for field use in control schemes. New drugs with reduced side-effects and greater efficiency are now being produced but it is too early to assess their value for control work. Attempts have been made to use some of the older less efficient compounds in suppressive therapy with the dose reduced to a level that does not give bad side-effects but greatly reduces the output of viable eggs by the worms. However, in a trial scheme using experimental animals, Jordan (1965) has shown that where levels of miracidial contamination are near to the maximum for a particular habitat, a 50% reduction in miracidial output only reduces the snail infection rate by 25%. The consequent lowering of cercarial output has a negligible effect in reducing the infection rate of experimental animals exposed in the habitat. A combination of mollusciciding and drug treatment is more likely to produce a reasonable degree of control than can be achieved by either approach on its own.

However, from the long-term point of view it must be realized that these measures require continual supervision by trained staff and the repeated use of expensive chemicals and drugs over long periods. To turn to the original basis of control—the elimination of contacts between infected people and snail-infested waters—it is obvious that a direct approach along these lines would have the greatest effect. The physical and psychological problems involved in implementing such schemes are enormous, but if successful the results would be permanent, and not only schistosomiasis but many other protozoan and helminth diseases would be eliminated. It is no good rushing into such programmes without a great deal of previous study. The provision of piped water supplies and sanitary facilities in the forms normally used in sophisticated societies may be quite unacceptable to rural communities, and they are often impractical in operation so that they cease to function soon after their installation.

This should not, however, be used as an argument against further attempts to seek acceptable and practical systems. The fact that such measures would have little general effect for many years to come is not a valid reason for further delay in their inception. Rather it should be a pressing incentive to start as soon as possible and so shorten the inevitable lapse of time before some lasting success is achieved. The eventual control of schistosomiasis will be in the hands of those who at present suffer from the disease. They will need guidance on how this can be achieved, but if the advice which is given is incompatible with local economic development it is likely to go unheeded (Wright, 1969).

References

AZIM, A. M. and GISMAN, A. (1956) Bilharziasis survey in South-western Asia. *Bull. Wld. Hlth. Org.*, **14**, 403–56.

BIGGS, H. E. J. (1960) Mollusca from prehistoric Jericho. *J. Conch. Lond.*, **24** (11), 379–87.

BROWN, D. S. and WRIGHT, C. A. (1974) *Bulinus truncatus* as a potential intermediate host for *Schistosoma haematobium* on the Kano Plain, Kenya. *Trans. roy. Soc. trop. Med. Hyg.*, **68**, 341–342.

COLE, S. (1964) *The Prehistory of East Africa*. Weidenfeld & Nicholson, London.

DEKKER, G. (1965) Climate and water resources in Africa, in *Ciba Foundation Symposium "Man in Africa"*. Edited by WOLSTENHOLME and O'CONNOR, Churchill, London, pp. 30–56.

FRIPP, P. J. (1963) Studies on *Schistosoma rhodaini* Brumpt, a trematode allied to *S. mansoni*. *Biochem. J.*, **89** (2), 74.

GIRGES, R. (1934) *Schistosomiasis*. J. Bale, Sons & Danielsson, London.

JORDAN, P. (1963) Some quantitative aspects of bilharzia with particular reference to suppressive therapy and mollusciciding in control of *S. haematobium* in Sukumaland, Tanganyika. *E. Afr. Med. J.*, **40** (5), 250–60.

JORDAN, P. (1965) Some observations on control of bilharziasis by chemotherapy. *E. Afr. Med. J.*, **42** (11), 614–19.

KUNTZ, R. E. (1952) *Schistosoma mansoni* and *S. haematobium* in the Yemen, Southwest Arabia: with a report of an unusual factor in the epidemiology of schistosomiasis mansoni. *J. Parasit.*, **38** (1), 24–8.

LAST, G. C. (1965) The geographical implications of man and his future in Africa, in *Ciba Foundation Symposium "Man in Africa"*. Edited by WOLSTENHOLME and O'CONNOR, Churchill, London, pp. 6–23.

LEAKEY, R. E. F. (1973) Australopithecines and hominines: a summary on the evidence from the early Pleistocene of Eastern Africa. In *The Concepts of Human Evolution*, ed. S. ZUCKERMAN. *Symp. Zool. Soc. Lond.*, **33**, 53–69.

LERICHE, M. (1925) Les fossiles du calcaire lacustre observè recemment sur le plateau du Kundelungu (Katanga). *Rev. Zool. Africaine*, **13** (1), 150–5.

PESIGAN, T. P., HAIRSTON, N. G., JAUREGUI, J. J., GARCIA, E. G., SANTOS, A. T., SANTOS, B. C. and BESA, A. A. (1958) Studies on *Schistosoma japonicum* infection in the Phillipines. 2, The molluscan host. *Bull. Wld. Hlth. Org.*, **18**, 481–578.

RUFFER, M. A. (1910) Note on the presence of *Bilharzia haematobia* in Egyptian mummies of the twentieth dynasty (1250–1000 B.C.). *Brit. Med. J.*, **1**, 16 (1910).

SHIFF, C. J. (1969) Influence of light and depth on location of *Bulinus* (*Plysopsis*) *globosus* by miracidia of Schistosoma haematobium. *J. Parasitol.*, **55**, 108–110.

SHIFF, C. J. (1974) Seasonal factors influencing the location of *Bulinus* (*Plysopsis*) *globosus* by miracidia of *Schistosoma haematobium* in nature. *J. Parasitol.*, **60**, 578–583.

SOUTHGATE, V. R. and KNOWLES, R. J. (in press) The intermediate hosts of *Schistosoma bovis* in Western Kenya. *Trans. roy. Soc. trop. Med. Hyg.*

WAJDI, N. (1972) Behaviour of the miracidia of an Iraqi strain of *Schistosoma haematobium*. *Bull. Wld. Hlth. Org.*, **46**, 115–117.

WRIGHT, C. A. (1960) Some ecological aspects of the control of trematode diseases. *W.H.O. Bilharz*, **39**, 1–5.

WRIGHT, C. A. (1961) Taxonomic problems in the molluscan genus *Bulinus*. *Trans. roy. Soc. Med. Hyg.*, **55** (3), 225–31.

WRIGHT, C. A. (1962) The significance of infra-specific taxonomy in bilharziasis, in *Ciba Foundation Symposium "Bilharziasis"*, edited by WOLSTENHOLME and O'CONNOR, Churchill, London, pp. 103–20.

WRIGHT, C. A. (1963) Schistosomiasis in the Western Aden Protectorate; a preliminary study. *Trans. roy. Soc. trop. Med. Hyg.*, **57** (2), 142–7.

WRIGHT, C. A. (1966) Relationships between schistosomes and their molluscan hosts in Africa. *J. Helminth.*, **40** (3/4), 403–12.

WRIGHT, C. A. (1969) Some biological views on the control of schistosomiasis. *Trans. roy. Soc. trop. Med. Hyg.*, **63** (supplement), 77–81.

WRIGHT, C. A. (1971) *Bulinus* on Aldabra and the subfamily Bulininae in the Indian Ocean area. *Phil. Trans. Roy. Soc. Lond.* B, **260**, 299–313.

WRIGHT, C. A., SOUTHGATE, V. R. and KNOWLES, R. J. (1972) What is *Schistosoma intercalatum*, Fisher, 1934? *Trans. roy. Soc. trop. Med. Hyg.*, **66** (1), 28–64.

INTERACTIONS BETWEEN HUMAN SOCIETIES AND VARIOUS TRYPANOSOME-TSETSE-WILD FAUNA COMPLEXES

J. FORD

I PROPOSE to describe the interaction between the trypanosome-tsetse-wild fauna ecosystem and the surrounding human communities of southern Busoga in Uganda and then to compare it with four other interactions. The people concerned are the Soga themselves, then the Sukuma who are also mixed farmers, but live in a drier climate south of Lake Victoria, and two pastoral societies, the Hima of the interlake area west of Victoria and the Fulani of West Africa. In addition some points are emphasized by reference to communities in Rhodesia. I have chosen these examples partly because I have had personal acquaintance with their problems, partly because they cover a fairly wide spectrum of African environments, and partly because for each there is a good range of scientific and other documentation.

It is convenient to begin with the Soga because they were involved in the terrible sleeping sickness epidemic in Uganda between 1901 and 1908 in which some 200 000 died out of a population at risk of about 300 000 (Cook, 1945). In 1890 southern Busoga was densely populated and covered with banana gardens (Thomas and Scott, 1935). The first cases of sleeping sickness were diagnosed in 1901. It was estimated that 20 000 Soga died in 1902 and by 1905 the total of deaths had risen to 100 000. The survivors were evacuated in 1906 and the banana gardens gave way to forest-savanna mosaic which became populated with elephant, buffalo and various other animals including bushbuck and bushpig and their attendant parasites (Mackichan, 1944). The evacuation halted the epidemic and the disease eventually died out in Busoga proper, although it

145

persisted in two foci near its eastern border and in Kenya. In 1939 infection appeared again and by mid-1943 there had been 2432 cases of which 10% were fatal. (By this time drugs for treatment of early cases were available and medical services were better organized.) The epidemic began among labourers on a sugar estate at the western end of the Busoga fly-belt, and moved rapidly eastwards through villages on its northern periphery and by 1942 had crossed the Kenya border 80 kilometres away. About this time it reached its peak, with some 100 cases monthly, but thereafter died away to a level of less than ten a month. Again infection disappeared first from western Busoga, but continued at a fairly high level of endemicity in the Lumino–Bwale area on the eastern border. The population of Busoga in 1959 stood at 660 000 (*Uganda Atlas*, 1962).

The epidemic of 1901 was caused by infected *Glossina fuscipes* (then called *G. palpalis*), a tsetse-fly which can flourish in the presence of dense human population, provided there are narrow galleries of riverine or lacustrine forest. The causal trypanosome was identified with the West African *Trypanosoma gambiense* and was supposed to have been introduced in 1890 by the Stanley–Emin Pasha expedition. The 1940 epidemic was, however, of a more acute disease and the causal trypanosome was *T. rhodesiense*, hitherto associated with the *Brachystegia* woodlands of Tanzania and its southern neighbours.

A second species of tsetse-fly, *Glossina pallidipes*, was recorded in Busoga in 1903. Later a third, *G. brevipalpis*, was found. There is no precise information about this early record of *G. pallidipes* and it did not interest the medical authorities until it was shown, in 1943, that it was probably the principal vector of the trypanosome responsible for this second epidemic. When it was found in 1903 it seems very likely that it (and *G. brevipalpis*) was living in small relic patches of forest and thicket associated with a range of low hills that forms the watershed between the Victoria and Kyoga drainages and that the present Busoga forests developed from their expansion after the 1906 evacuation. In 1943 it was thought that the trypanosome was introduced by immigrant labourers from Tanzania. But what puzzled everybody was why the epidemic died down after mid-1942 when little had been done to implement any control other than treatment of patients (Mackichan, 1944). Early in 1944 I was sent to Busoga to carry out a survey of the distribution of *Glossina pallidipes*. On its results a scheme was to be devised to break the contact between the human population and the tsetse-infested forests. Like everyone else concerned (except the Soga) I was convinced that this was an urgent matter, if a recrudescence of the epidemic was to be prevented. However, the Soga refused to collaborate in the reorganization of land occupation that we thought so desirable. They were right and we were wrong, for nothing happened, with one exception which must now be briefly described.

In 1957 the endemic condition that had persisted since 1943 showed signs of again becoming epidemic. In 1954, 1955 and 1956 new cases had appeared at a rate of about seven per month. Robertson (1963) showed that in 1957 the rate doubled. Shortly before this happened the lake fishing industry had been reorganized; outboard motors replaced paddles, flax nets were replaced by nylon, and more fishing licences were issued. The increase in the fishing population meant that more persons were at risk of infection. It also meant that there were more contacts between infected people and the lake shore populations of *Glossina fuscipes*, which now became involved, as well as *G. pallidipes*, in the transmission of *Trypanosoma rhodesiense*. Some control over movement to the lake shore was instituted and the medical service continued to work efficiently, so that although the annual incidence of sleeping sickness rose there was no disruptive epidemic.

To return now to the problems of why the 1940 epidemic began and why, two years later, it died down. In 1944 I mapped a line that enclosed nearly 1680 square km of tsetse-infested country, bounded in the south by the lake shore and in the north by more densely populated cultivated land. One could not relate the outline of forest and thicket to the limits of tsetse. The notion of a forest-savanna mosaic fits the Busoga vegetation well. Cultivation starts on the savanna interstices and eats into the forest, so that between the fully inhabited and the uninhabited area is a zone in which the ratio of cultivation plus savanna to forest is at first high, but becomes progressively less, with the forest part of the mosaic becoming greater as one moves towards the lake away from the outer, fully occupied, land. Somewhere in this zone one encounters tsetse-flies. In 1965 I revisited Busoga and it seemed that the fly-line had retreated. Mr. J. M. B. Harley, then of the East African Trypanosomiasis Research Organization, repeated my survey over a portion of the fly-front and a comparison of his 1966 map with mine of 1944 makes it clear that *G. pallidipes* had receded by about 8 km. It seems likely that the area infested by tsetses west of the Kenya border had been halved in the 22-year interval. A. G. Robertson, (1957) estimated that the Busoga fly-belt was reduced by about 260 square km between 1951 and 1956.

One difficulty in studying African epidemiology is that there are no reliable indices of population growth before 1948. In some countries, however, we are better off when we turn to the cattle, not only because counts or estimates were made quite frequently, but also because, although we do not know how many cattle there were at the beginning of the century, we do know that in most areas about 95% of the cattle population died in the rinderpest panzootic between 1890 and 1900. The cattle population was reduced as near to zero as it could be without disappearing altogether. Subsequent trends seem highly probable, which is more than can be said for most of the pre-1948 human data.

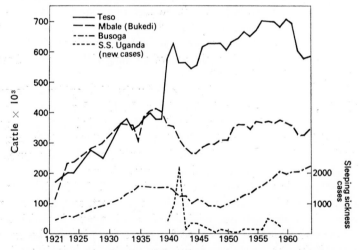

Fig. 1. Cattle populations of Busoga, Mbale and Teso districts and the numbers of new cases of sleeping sickness in Uganda from 1940 onwards, nearly all of them from Busoga and Mbale districts. (From Ford, 1971, by permission of the Clarendon Press).

Figure 1 shows growth curves for the cattle populations of Busoga and its neighbouring districts of Mbale and Teso, from 1921 to 1964, as well as the numbers of cases of human trypanosomiasis from

1940 to 1959. Busoga cattle live in relatively close contact with the fly-belt; most of the Mbale cattle are further away, while Teso cattle have little contact with tsetse-flies. Throughout Uganda from 1920 onwards, cattle generally were increasing rapidly until the mid-thirties. In Busoga cattle numbers stopped increasing around 1935; in Mbale the decline began in 1938. However, during this period the stock population of Teso was greatly augmented and it is clear that this was due to immigration from the districts in which the fly-belts lay.

The rapid growth of the cattle population in Uganda, as in East Africa as a whole, from 1920 onwards, reflected recovery from the rinderpest. The interruption of the upward trend was due to their collision with the fly-belts which, in Uganda, were released from confinement behind settlement by the sleeping sickness evacuations between 1906 and 1914. Figure 2 compares outlines of tsetse distribution in 1933 (Uganda, *Annual Report*, Department of Veterinary

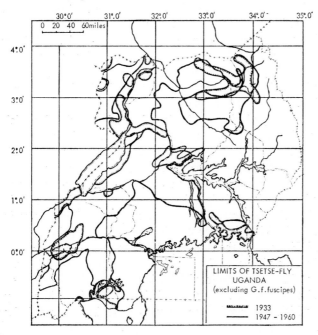

FIG. 2. Limits of tsetse-flies (excluding *Glossina f. fuscipes*) in Uganda in 1933 and maximum extension of the fly-belts between 1947 and 1960.

Services) and its greatest extension between 1947 and 1960 (*Annual Reports*, Department of Tsetse Control).

In Busoga the collision between the expanding cattle population and the fly bush resulted in a reduction from 158 000 head in 1935 to 88 500 in 1949 (*Annual Reports*, Department of Veterinary Services, also Watson, 1954). As elsewhere this trend was reversed after the introduction of mass drug treatment in 1950. Our chief interest in Fig. 1 lies in its demonstration that the epidemic which built up among the people so rapidly in 1941 and 1942 occurred while the cattle were diminishing in number as a result of tsetse-borne infection. There are no figures for incidence of cattle trypanosomiasis before 1949, but in that year a blood slide survey showed 11·0% infected with *Trypanosoma congolense*, 5·8% with *T. vivax* and 2·9% with *T. brucei*. It was the first two of these parasites that were killing off the cattle. The third, which to them is harmless, includes those strains which cause sleeping sickness in man and which are properly called *Trypanosoma brucei rhodesiense*. All are transmitted by tsetse bite. It was thought that the human infection must have been brought in from Tanzania. But the cattle trypanosomes certainly came from the wild animals in the Busoga forests and so, one must believe, did those infecting the people. A number of investigations have since provided evidence to support this view.

In 1964 an explosive epidemic of Rhodesian sleeping sickness flared up in Alego in Kenya, about 32 km from both the Uganda border and the lake shore. Only *Glossina fuscipes* was found, not only along the rivers, but living in the villages in hedges and bushes around the kraals and gardens and feeding on people and on their domestic animals. This invasion of villages by hitherto riverine or lacustrine flies seems to have been associated with the rise in the level of Lake Victoria after the abnormally heavy rains of 1961–62. The chief interest of the Alego epidemic comes from the demonstration that the village cattle were infected with *T. rhodesiense*. They thus provided a reservoir of infection actually in the villages and immediately available for transmission to the inhabitants by the tsetses which also lived there (Onyango, van Hoeve and de Raadt, 1966).

In 1971 an entire Soga family of six persons was found to be infected with *Trypanosoma rhodesiense*. They lived near the village of Busesa about 8 kilometres outside the south Busoga forest, but got their water, for themselves and their cattle, from streams infested with *Glossina fuscipes*. The blood was examined of 800 cattle in the neighbourhood and 78 strains of *T. brucei*-like trypanosomes were obtained of which 10 were later identified as *T. rhodesiense* (Mwambu *et al.*, 1971). At the same time 394 *Glossina fuscipes* were examined and 19 *T. brucei* type infections were obtained, of which four were later identified as *T. rhodesiense*. The infection rate in these tsetses by trypanosomes possibly infective to man was one of the highest ever recorded (Rogers *et al.*, 1971). That the six patients had been infected by flies which had obtained their own infections from cattle seems very likely.

Another study which illuminates the Busoga problem has been made in part of the Samia location which lies between the Kenya-Uganda border and Alego. The greater part of the people lives near the lake shore or along the Sio River, which is the international boundary. Wijers (1974) has recorded with great care the probable sites in which 112 people who lived in this part of Samia had become infected between 1955 and 1968. Ninety of them lived in the so-called "lake area" which is bounded on the west by the shore. This is infested with *Glossina fuscipes*, which is also found along the Sio River which bounds the "river area". The eastern border of the "lake area" is formed by the Busia range of hills. The footslopes of these hills are covered by extensive thickets in which live wild animals, including bushbuck and wild pig, which support an infestation of *Glossina pallidipes*. Of the 90 "lake area" dwellers 37 were fishermen of whom 19 were doubtful about where they had become infected. Seven thought they had acquired the disease outside Samia, but 11 believed themselves to have been infected near home. Of 23 male cultivators all said they had been infected near home, as did 24 women cultivators. Six children must also have been infected at home. When Wijers plotted the precise positions of the homes of these people it became clear that they nearly all lived, not in the more densely populated parts near the *G. fuscipes* infested shore, but around the periphery of the thickets in which lived *Glossina pallidipes* and the wild animals on which the flies lived. In many cases they had felled areas of thicket to make their gardens. No cattle were kept near these thickets. Wijers concluded that these

L

inhabitants of Samia had acquired the greater part of their infections by direct bite of *G. pallidipes*.

There are evidently a number of routes by which *T. rhodesiense* may leave their natural hosts and establish themselves in human beings. The latter, like the cultivators of the Samia "lake area" or the villagers living around the edge of the Busoga forest in 1940–1943, may be bitten by *Glossina pallidipes* which have become infected by feeding on their natural hosts. *Glossina fuscipes* may also play this role. In either event the human victim is likely to live in close proximity to, or to have entered, the habitat of the wild host. But when the epidemic occurs in villages some miles away from wild animal habitats it seems most likely, as Wilde and French (1945) suggested long ago, that the trypanosomes have been carried by cattle, in which they are harmless and which form a reservoir from which, for many months, domesticated tsetses, like *G. fuscipes* at Alego or at Busesa, may become infected.

The events leading to an outbreak of sleeping sickness may be very complex. I have given no account, in the foregoing, of the diversity of response made by different tsetses to different hosts nor have I mentioned the immune processes in both natural and adventitious host animals which may influence the course of infection and so on.

After the alarm created in 1957 by the augmented level of infection following changes in the pattern of the fishing industry, it was not surprising that there was disagreement about what should be done (Robertson, 1963; Morris, 1960). Some advocated encouragement of settlement penetration inside the forest edge, because this would be followed by a withdrawal of the wild mammal population and a retreat of *G. pallidipes*. Others claimed that this would increase the incidence of infection. Both were right and, in a sense, both were wrong. The higher incidence of sleeping sickness since 1957 demonstrated that settlers could not penetrate the fly-belt with impunity; but equally there was no doubt that the expanding population was repeating what it had done at least once before in its history: it was destroying the natural ecosystem and replacing it by one that was man-made.

Figure 3 shows successive stages in the replacement of the trypanosome-tsetse-wild fauna ecosystem by the mixed farming society of

Sukuma, who are by far the most important cattle-owning community in Tanzania. Whatever may have been the west-to-east limits of Sukumaland, Stanley's evidence of 1876 shows that its north-to-south dimensions were at least as great as in 1947, while on another line further west Speke's 1854 traverse demonstrates that open country with cattle-owning inhabitants was more or less continuous from Mwanza to Tabora (160 kilometres south of Shinyanga). The area around Shinyanga was much depopulated by wars in the eighties and Emin Pasha, on his way south in 1891, described settlements a few miles across alternating with bush populated by wild animals, including buffalo (Stuhlmann, 1916–27). Shortly after this the rinderpest panzootic began the series of biological and social catastrophes which accompanied the European invasion over much of the continent. The buffalo around Shinyanga, like giraffe north of Lake George, were exterminated and never returned. A not very accurate vegetation map compiled by the German botanist Engler (Meyer, 1909) shows that some 15 years later, at about the latitude of Shinyanga, *Brachystegia* woodland from the west and *Acacia-Commiphora* steppe from the east joined in a band perhaps 48 km wide. When Swynnerton (1925) collected information about the history of the Shinyanga area he found that in 1913 tsetse-fly was only known near Nindo, which was the one area noted by Speke in 1854 as having been "jungle" populated by wild animals. It was evidently a classic example of a "natural focus of infection" of the kind described by Russian epidemiologists (Pavlovskii, 1963).

I made a first version of Fig. 3 in 1948 and showed that within the limits shown, tsetse-infested areas had diminished by some 9000 square kilometres since 1925, and that the central cultivated portion had expanded by the same amount. It was disconcerting, at that time, to find that only 2000 square kilometres of the area freed from infestation could be attributed to specifically anti-tsetse measures. The expansion is still going on and the fly-free area, which in 1925 was under 15 500, is now over 40 000 square kilometres in area. The population curve for the Sukuma cattle is similar in form to that of Busoga, but the halt in recovery from the rinderpest came earlier, with a sharp drop in numbers in 1932. Recovery also came earlier. In Busoga it was the introduction of new drugs in 1950 that reversed the trend. In Sukumaland the reversal took place during the

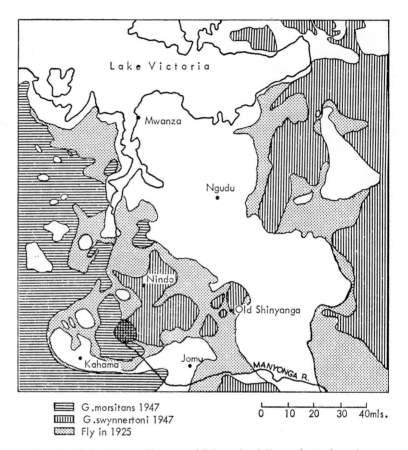

G.morsitans 1947
G.swynnertoni 1947
Fly in 1925

0   10   20   30   40mls.

FIG. 3. Limits of tsetse-flies around Sukumaland, Tanzania, to show the
retreat of the fly-belts between 1925 and 1947.

war years and was a response to the extra pasture that early efforts
in tsetse control and, later, the expanding human population were
already providing. In general where the tsetse involved are *G.
morsitans* or closely related species like *G. swynnertoni*, trypanosomiasis is not a major factor controlling numbers of East African
cattle. It does, however, control the amount of pasture available and
this provides the main limitation on cattle numbers. This is well
demonstrated by African owned cattle in Rhodesia (Fig. 4). Here,
at least to 1950 and then only to a minor degree, pasture did not

adjoin the fly-belts. Fences kept the cattle from using pasture on European lands. The data are very complete from 1897 and fluctuations in the curve of annual increment are attributable either to droughts, which reduce grazing, or to imposed regulations compelling de-stocking. But the form of the curve is the same as in countries further north where the fly belts limit the grazing lands (Chief Native Commissioner Reports, 1901–62).

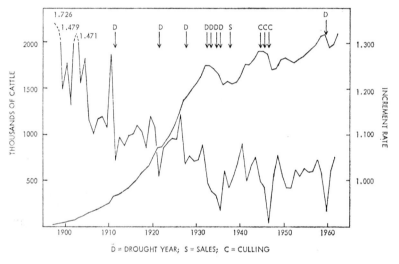

FIG. 4. African-owned cattle in Rhodesia. Population growth, annual increment rates, and years in which climate and other controlling agencies had noticeable effects.

Quite recently much light has been thrown upon the role of the human infection in controlling expansion east of Sukumaland. In 1922 it was found that people living around the *G. swynnertoni* fly-bush east of Ngudu (Fig. 3) were moving into the fly-free central area to escape sleeping sickness. The story has been described elsewhere (Ford, 1971), but a new chapter has now been added. Just off the north-east corner of the area shown in Fig. 3 lies the great Serengeti National Park. The 1922 epidemic finally died away in 1954. In 1964 two cases of sleeping sickness were notified, one of them an employee at the National Park Headquarters. By 1969 there had been 31 cases among which were two tourists. A comprehensive survey was carried out by the East African Trypasosomiasis

Research Organization and the Swiss Tropical Institute. It was established beyond any doubt that human infective trypanosomes, *T. rhodesiense*, were present in many of the wild animals and in cattle owned by villagers at Ikoma just outide the Park boundary (Onyango and Woo; Geigy, Mwambu and Kauffman; Mwambu and Mayende, 1971, and other papers). The most recent publication of the series is that of Moloo and Kutuza (1974) who conclude that "there are no restricted foci of Rhodesian sleeping sickness but rather the various components comprising zoonosis interact sporadically throughout this part of Tanzania". From this it follows that the major factor affecting incidence of the disease is the frequency of man-fly contact. This is likely to be high in situations where there is a high tsetse density associated with permanent occupation by wild animals which is situated in close proximity to a sufficiently dense human population. The vital factor, perhaps, in the generally rather arid area around the Serengeti Park, is the presence in the Ikoma region of the relatively large Grumeti and Orangi River drainage which supplies permanent water for people, the cattle and non-migrant wild animals. Moloo and Kutuza have stated an important principle which needs further study in relation to other places having a long history of continuous or recurrent infection.

If the examples of Busoga and Sukumaland have shown human societies in the last quarter century to have been winning in the confrontation with the wild-life ecosystems, this cannot be said of the semi-nomadic Hima society of Ankole in western Uganda. Figure 5 (based partly on maps by Lambrecht, 1955 and Buyckx, 1962) illustrates the invasion by *G. morsitans* of the interlake area west of Victoria that began between 1890 and 1900 and continued in south-western Uganda, in Rwanda and in Burundi, at any rate until 1960, in spite of quite massive efforts to prevent it. I want to draw attention to two features of this interaction. When I began to study it many years ago a puzzling feature was that, although all evidence supported the view that *G. morsitans* was a new arrival and that the disease it carried had been hitherto unknown, there was some evidence of another long-established disease of cattle, having another name, which also seemed to have been bovine trypanosomiasis. We identified three localities associated with this disease. It will be seen that they all lie in the path of the early, very rapid spread of *G. morsitans* between, perhaps, 1895 and 1925. This spread

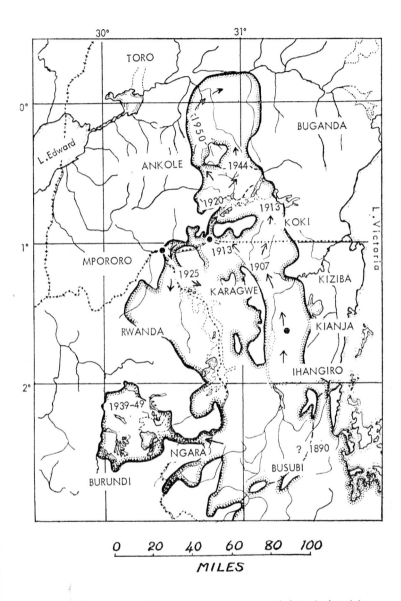

FIG. 5. The spread of *Glossina morsitans* westwards into the interlake zone after the rinderpest panzootic of 1891, with the principal kingdoms at that date and three historical foci of trypanosomiasis probably transmitted by *G. pallidipes*,

was very rapid because the tsetse was able to occupy country already carrying natural savanna and woodland communities inhabited by suitable wild animal hosts.

The Germans in Tanzania had recognized that African kingdoms and tribal areas were often separated from one another by a no-man's land for which they coined the name of *Grenzwildnis*— "boundary wilderness". These zones were associated with natural features of the landscape, often those which made the land they occupy not very suitable for human exploitation, and sometimes they had a strategic value for military defence. In the inter-lake areas they also had a function in succession wars. When the divine king died, the sons who failed to secure possession of the royal drums, but still wanted to fight for them, fled to the *Grenzwildnis* and thence waged war against their brother, the new king. Also, of course, these boundary zones provided habitats for *Glossina pallidipes* and *G. brevipalpis*, flies that can persist in quite restricted localities, because their favoured hosts are also restricted. When the social collapses which followed the European invasion permitted *G. morsitans* to break through the barriers of settlement which had, until then, confined that species to the *Brachystegia* woodlands further south, they became paths for its rapid spread into new country. Finally they provided a grazing reserve used in times of stress, but often dangerous because of the latent potential for trypanosome infection which was, however, usually attributed to supposedly poisonous plants in certain recognized places which were, if possible, to be avoided. These areas are also "natural foci of infection" of the Russian school.

The second point about this spread of *G. morsitans* is also concerned with its speed. It was halted in 1919 by a severe rinderpest epizootic that killed off most of the population of wild host animals. In 1925 it began again, but rather more slowly until in 1940 it slowed down to a mere northward trickle along the western edge of the dry-grass savanna of north-east Ankole. This continued for ten years and then, quite suddenly, between 1953 and 1958, about 1800 square kilo-metres of pasture became flooded with tsetse, which occupied the whole of the remaining dry savanna of Ankole and began to invade what was left of this particular vegetation in the neighbouring kingdom of Buganda.

Ten years earlier we had not been worried about the spread of tsetse-fly into this part of Ankole. Although it was evident that it could happen one day, we thought that by that time we should have the situation under control. Nevertheless we gave much thought to the growth of trees, particularly of *Acacia hockii* and *A. gerrardii* which were beginning to invade these grasslands. We blamed the foresters for having brought in a new policy of grass burning; we blamed the Hima for their methods of pasture control; we blamed the advancing tsetse-flies for having occupied the southern pastures and upset the traditional pattern of transhumance.

It is certain that the ecological causes of the invasion of the north-eastern Ankole pasture by *Acacia* and the population of the resulting savanna by wild animals, trypanosomes and tsetses were very complex, but we missed, as I now think, the principal cause. Because of intensive hunting, elephants ceased to migrate annually through the Ankole grasslands in 1937. For many years their bones lay in the grass. In 1923 a herd of about a hundred elephants was seen sharing a water-hole with 400 head of cattle in north-eastern Ankole (Swynnerton, 1923) and we have a reliable description (Garstin, 1904) of the destruction by elephants in 1904 of the trees, which at that time were confined to a narrow band around the foothills that bound these pastures on the south and west. Elephants, aided by fire, have, in recent years, eliminated tsetse-flies from large parts of two of the East African national parks by destroying trees (Ford, 1966) and it seems probable that a major factor in the spread of *G. morsitans* into the northern Ankole pastures between 1955 and 1960 was the elephant slaughter 20 to 30 years before. This released a succession of vegetation and fauna which, by the mid-fifties, had reached a condition in which *Glossina* suddenly found an adequate food supply and suitable habitat where hitherto it had found neither.

The semi-nomadic life of the Hima pastoralists has almost disappeared under the influences of shrinking pasture caused by the take-over by the trypanosome-tsetse-wild life ecosystem and then, when that was finally dealt with, by the efforts of government to encourage mixed farming or pasturing in enclosed ranches and lastly, by the political overthrow of the kingship which, for centuries, had belonged to the cattle-keeping overlords. The reaction of the Hima to infection had always been to run away; the Sukuma, on the other hand, in times of drought, deliberately pastured their cattle in tsetse-infested bush, saying that although they would lose many from infection, starvation on the exhausted pastures around their homes would take all. The Fulani of West Africa take this process a step further and every year take hundreds of thousands of cattle on a long annual migration from the home pastures in the northern Sudan and southern Sahel vegetation regions, which are largely outside the limits of tsetse, into the fly-infested Guinea zones. They avoid the more heavily infested belts of *G. morsitans* but, although there are appreciable losses from trypanosomiasis, it is evident that, by virtue of this repeated contact with infection, the Fulani cattle have acquired a much greater tolerance of trypanosomes than have most East African cattle and that, from the point of view of stock increase, the losses by trypanosomiasis are outweighed by the benefits of the annual transhumance.

Again, recent events force one to revise the picture. Over the last decade the climate of the Sahel has been going through a cyclical phase of greater than usual dryness (Dalby and Harrison Church, 1973). The dreadful famines which have ensued have brought death to hundreds of thousands of people and their livestock. It is difficult to avoid the conclusion that modern veterinary medicine as well as projects such as drilling of boreholes for water, which were intended to increase productivity, have appreciably reduced the ability of the Sahel populations to adjust to unusual dryness: indeed, they must have exacerbated its effect. Two diseases which, in the past, have helped to keep the reproductive potential of the cattle in adjustment with the limited resources of the environment have been rinderpest and trypanosomiasis. The first has been virtually eliminated over the last ten years as a result of a continentally-wide vaccination campaign; the effects of trypanosomiasis, which include not only death and disease, but also reduce the normal calving rate, have largely been removed by massive use, since the mid-fifties, of modern drugs. In the past death and low fertility caused by infections have helped to achieve a balance with the Sahel environment; with their removal, starvation takes over the ecological task.

To the glossinologist tropical Africa is divided into the area draining into the Indian Ocean, from which tsetse-flies of the *palpalis* group are absent, and areas draining into the Atlantic and Mediterranean in which they are present and infest most river banks and lake shores where there is suitable vegetation to harbour them.

Busoga and Ankole fall into this area, but only the northern part of Sukumaland. Flies of the *palpalis* group readily feed off man and therefore, as already noted, persist in areas of relatively dense population. Flies of the *morsitans* group are found in the savanna and deciduous woodland vegetation zones of Africa from Mozambique to Senegal. They turn much less readily to man for their food and tend to be eliminated by extensive, dense, human settlement. A third group, the *fusca* group, is found chiefly in and around the forests of the Zaire basin and in West Africa.

In discussing Busoga I noted that two varieties of human trypanosomiasis were recognized. West African sleeping sickness is caused by *Trypanosoma gambiense* and kills slowly. One supposes, therefore, that it is better adjusted to an environment of human blood than is *T. rhodesiense* which kills quickly. Duggan (1962) suggested that the better adjusted *T. gambiense* may have evolved in the drier woodlands and savannas of West Africa. Here *G. morsitans* overlaps extensively the river systems infested with *palpalis*-group flies. The Lake Chad basin is one in which *rhodesiense*-like trypanosomes were found. Duggan supposed that here persons may become infested by such trypanosomes, especially from bushbuck, a proven reservoir of *T. rhodesiense*, by a bite of *G. morsitans*. These persons would infect *palpalis*-group flies which would in turn disseminate infection to large human populations, thus providing a means whereby strains of trypanosomes best adapted to man would be selected for survival and so give rise to the widely distributed *T. gambiense*. One objection to this is that the overlap of *G. morsitans*, *palpalis*-group tsetses, and bushbuck extends far south into the more humid Niger-Benue valley, which is a principal focus of chronic *T. gambiense* and where *rhodesiense*-like epidemics do not occur. However, Duggan's idea would still hold good if *G. morsitans* in the dry north attacked man more readily than it did in the wet south. There were reasons for supposing this might be so. At Ilorin, south of the River Niger, it was found that in the dry season *Glossina morsitans* bit a bait ox once every 12 minutes, whereas bites on men occurred only once in 105 minutes. The corresponding figures in the much more arid environment of the Yankari Game Reserve were 12 and 11 minutes. In the wet season similar results were obtained. Thus, other things being equal, man in the northern environment seems to be almost nine times more susceptible to *morsitans* bites than in the south

(Ford, 1969). We now know that *T. gambiense* and *T. rhodesiense* differ in composition of their DNA content and thus, presumably, are genetically separate (Newton and Burnett, 1966). However, Duggan's hypothesis as to the means whereby trypanosomes which are essentially blood parasites of wild animals may be transferred to and achieve relative stability in human hosts, seems to have a sound entomological foundation.

It is worth noting, although so far we can do no more than note, that the most extensive and massively destructive human epidemics tend to take place around the periphery of the Zaire basin and the West African forests (of which the Busoga forest is a small eastward extension). Here *palpalis*-group tsetses overlap with either *morsitans*-group or with *fusca*-group tsetses, or with both. In these zones there must be maximal opportunity for trypanosomes circulating in numerous transmission paths involving several species of tsetse and several wild host animals to transfer either directly or via domestic animals to *palpalis*-group/man transmission cycles. It is precisely in these zones that human societies have constantly sought to convert the forest environment to one of agriculture and husbandry and it is here that the process of trypanosome adjustment to man takes place with greatest intensity.

I have tried to show that the ecology of trypanosomiasis is complex. In the great proliferation of books about Africa it is not uncommon to see references to the supposed effects of tsetse-fly. More than one eminent prehistorian has invoked *Glossina* as a controlling mechanism for Stone Age migrations. The evidence is flimsy. In West Africa breeds of cattle have developed which are tolerant of infection and dense human populations have grown up in spite of endemic sleeping sickness. In East Africa cattle populations have more than doubled during a period in which the fly-belts have expanded by many thousands of square miles. Almost all modern human ecology in tropical Africa has to be studied in the light of the catastrophic epidemics and epizootics which followed the European invasion and this applies equally to the social effects of trypanosomiasis.

References

BUYCKX, E. J. E. (1962) Rapport préliminaire sur la deuxième campagne de désinsectisation par voie aerienne contre *Glossina morsitans* Westwood au Bugesera. Mimeographed report of the I.N.E.A.C.—R.U. Mission Tsétsé Bugesera.

COOK, Sir Albert R. (1945) *Uganda Memories* (1897–1940), Kampala.
DALBY, D. and HARRISON CHURCH, R. J. (Editors) (1973) *Drought in Africa: Report of the 1973 Symposium*. Centre for African Studies, School of Oriental and African Studies, University of London.
DUGGAN, A. J. (1962) A survey of sleeping sickness in northern Nigeria from the earliest times to the present day. *Trans. Roy. Soc. trop. Med. Hyg.*, **56**, 56, 539–486.
FORD, J. (1966) The role of elephants in controlling the distribution of tsetse-flies. *I.U.C.N. Bulletin*, N.S., No. 19, 6.
FORD, J. (1969) Feeding and other responses of tsetse-flies to man and ox and their epidemiological significance. *Acta trop.*, **26**, 249–264.
FORD, J. (1971) *The role of the trypanosomiases in African ecology: A study of the tsetse-fly problem*. Clarendon Press, Oxford.
GARSTIN, SIR WILLIAM (1904) *Despatch from His Majesty's Agent and Consul-General at Cairo inclosing a report by Sir William Garstin, G.C.M.G. Under-Secretary of State for Public Works in Egypt, upon the Basin of the Upper Nile*. London, H.M.S.O. (Cmnd. 2165).
GEIGY, R., MWAMBU, P. M. and KAUFFMANN, M. (1971) Sleeping Sickness Survey in Musoma District, Tanzania. IV. Examination of Wild mammals as a potential reservoir for *T. rhodesiense*. *Acta trop.*, **28**, 211–220.
LAMBRECHT, F. L. (1955) Contribution a l'étude de la répartition des tsé-tsés dans les territoires du Ruanda-Urundi. *Ann. Soc. Belge Med. trop.*, **35**, 427–438.
MACKICHAN, I. W. (1944) Rhodesian sleeping sickness in eastern Uganda. *Trans. Roy. Soc. trop. Med. Hyg.*, **38**, 49–60.
MEYER, H. (1909) *Das deutsche Kolonialreich*. Leipzig.
MOLOO, S. K. and KUTUZA, S. B. (1974) Sleeping sickness survey in Musoma District, Tanzania: Further study on the vector role of *Glossina*. *Trans. Roy. Soc. trop. Med. Hyg.*, **68**, 403–409.
MORRIS, K. R. S. (1960) Trapping as a means of studying the game tsetse *Glossina pallidipes* Aust. *Bull. ent. Res.*, **51**, 533–557.
MWAMBU, P. M. and MAYENDE, J. S. P. (1971) Sleeping sickness survey in Musoma District, Tanzania: III. Survey of cattle for the evidence of *T. rhodesiense* infections. *Acta trop.*, **28**, 206–210.
MWAMBU, P. M., MAYENDE, J. S. P., MASINDE, A. and OMASET, P. A. (1971) Isolation of *T. brucei*-group organisms from cattle in Busoga District, Uganda, and drug sensitivity trials and B.I.I.T. on them. *E. African Trypanosomiasis Research Organization, Annual Report*. E. African Community, Government Printer, Entebbe, 40–44.
NEWTON, B. A. and BURNETT, J. K. (1972) The satellite DNA's of salivarian trypanosomes. *Trans. Roy. Soc. trop. Med. Hyg.*, **66**, 353–354.
ONYANGO, R. J., VAN HOEVE, K. and DE RAADT, P. (1966) The epidemiology of *Trypanosoma rhodesiense* sleeping sickness in Alego location, Central Nyanza, Kenya. 1. Evidence that cattle may act as reservoir hosts of trypanosomes infective to man. *Trans. Roy. Soc. trop. Med. Hyg.*, **60**, 175–182.
ONYANGO, R. J., and WOO, P. (1971) Sleeping sickness survey in Musoma District, Tanzania: Investigation of the incidence of sleeping sickness in the human population. *Acta trop.*, **28**, 181–188.
PAVLOVSKII, E. N. (Ed.) (1973) *Natural foci of human infections*. Jerusalem.
ROBERTSON, A. G. (1957) *Annual Report of the Tsetse Control Department*. Uganda Government Printer, Entebbe.
ROBERTSON, D. H. H. (1963) Human trypanosomiasis in South-eastern Uganda. A further study of the disease among fishermen and peasant cultivators. *Bull. Wld. Hlth. Org.*, **28**, 627–643.
ROGERS, A. (1972) A high infection rate of *Trypanosoma brucei* sub-group in *Glossina fuscipes*. *Parasitology*, **65**, 143–146.
SPEKE, J. H. (1864) *What led to the discovery of the source of the Nile*. Edinburgh.

STANLEY, H. M. (1878) *Through the dark continent*. London.
STUHLMANN, F. (1916–27) *Die Tagebücher von Dr. Emin Pascha*. Hamburg.
SWYNNERTON, C. F. M. (1923) *Report to the Uganda Protectorate Government on Elephants*. Typed draft, E.A.T.R.O., Archives, Tororo.
SWYNNERTON, C. F. M. (1925) An experiment in the control of tsetse-flies at Shinyanga, T.T. *Bull. ent. Res.*, **15**, 313–337.
THOMAS, H. B. and SCOTT, R. (1935) *Uganda*. London.
WATSON, T. Y. (1954) *Report of the Agricultural Productivity Committee*. Uganda Protectorate Government Printer, Entebbe.
WIJERS, D. J. B. (1974) The complex epidemiology of rhodesian sleeping sickness in Kenya and Uganda. Part II. Observations in Samia (Kenya). *Trop. geogr. Med.*, **26**, 182–197.
WILDE, J. K. H. and FRENCH, M. H. (1945) An experimental study of *Trypanosoma rhodesiense* infection in zebu cattle. *J. comp. Path.*, **55**, 206.

RESPONSE TO DROUGHT: THE MURSI OF SOUTHWESTERN ETHIOPIA

D. TURTON

THE Mursi are transhumant pastoralists and cultivators who number about 4000, and who occupy about 1540 sq km in the lower valley of the River Omo, in southwestern Ethiopia. This paper is a study of the way in which their social and economic organization is adapted to the exploitation of a marginal environment, in which there is a great deal of "fluctuation around mean conditions" (Johnson, 1973, p. 4). It is also offered as a contribution to the study of a subject which, following the severe drought and famine conditions which have afflicted the Sahel region of Africa in the last few years, has assumed great practical importance: response to drought. For, since my first visit to them in 1969–70, the Mursi have experienced their worst food shortage in living memory and, on returning for a further 12 months fieldwork in 1973, I was able to get some idea of the way in which they had responded to this period of extreme hardship[1].

The Mursi

Mursi country lies about 100 km north of Lake Rudolf, and is bordered to the west and south by the Omo, and to the east by its tributary the Mako, or Usno (Fig. 1). The Omo is a formidable river: it flows for 1000 km before entering Lake Rudolf, has a total

[1] Fieldwork was financed by grants from the Social Science Research Council of Great Britain, the Tweedie Exploration Fellowship Committee of the University of Edinburgh, the Central Research Fund of the University of London, and the Royal Geographical Society. I am grateful to all of these bodies for their generous assistance.

This paper originated as a talk to the Tropical Section of the British Ecological Society (April 8th, 1975). An earlier draft of it was read by Dr. P. T. W. Baxter Professor E. L. Peters and Dr. H. J. Blackhurst, to whom I am indebted for their valuable comments.

165

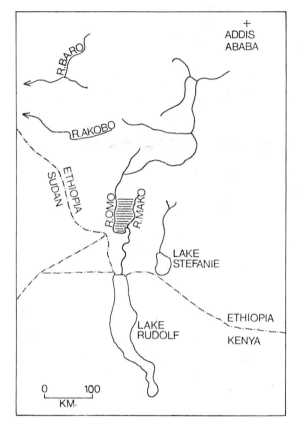

FIG. 1. The Location of Mursi Country.

catchment area of 73 000 sq km (Butzer, 1971, p. 3), and is between 150 and 200 metres wide in Mursi country. Another Omo tributary, smaller than the Mako and rarely in spate, forms the Mursi's northern boundary. This is the Mara, north of which live the Bodi who, in their way of life, language and culture are very similar to the Mursi. The two groups do not intermarry, however, and their languages are not mutually intelligible. Mursi country consists essentially of a volcanic upland, dissected by a large number of dry river beds (they may fill with water for a matter of days after heavy rain) and rising steadily eastwards from the Omo (approximately 500 metres above sea level at this latitude) towards the Mursi

Mountains, which reach a height of 1666 metres. This range, which, on existing maps, is known as "Ngallabong", from the Turkana name for the Mursi, forms the watershed between the Omo and Mako valleys (Fig. 2).

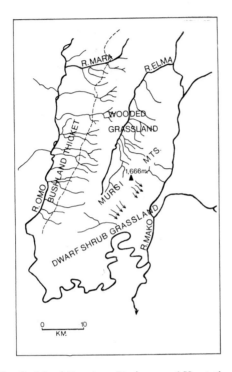

FIG. 2. Mursi Country : Drainage and Vegetation.

Largely because of their geographical position, the Mursi have been affected even less than other groups in this relatively little known part of Africa by the fact that their territory lies within the political boundaries of present-day Ethiopia. When I first visited them, most Mursi had not heard of Ethiopia, and only two could speak Amharic, the national language. They have received, to date, no regular provision of veterinary, medical, educational or agricultural services, nor are there any missionaries stationed permanently among them. (At the time of writing—June 1975—however, members of the

M

Sudan Interior Mission were preparing an airstrip in northern Mursi country, near the River Mara.) Administratively, Mursi country falls within the Hamar–Baco District of Gemu–Gofa Province. The administrative centre of Hamar–Baco is Jinka, a town with a resident governor and police commander, an airstrip, served regularly by Ethiopiam Airlines, and a twice weekly market. In normal times, however, the Mursi are not frequent visitors to Jinka, which lies only about 80 km to the east of them. This is largely because of the physical difficulties and dangers involved in crossing the Mako valley, which is an uninhabited "buffer" area between the Mursi and their inveterate enemies, the Hamar. The relative isolation of the Mursi is the first important point I wish to draw attention to, since, as will be seen later, it has a great deal to do with their ability to adapt to and recover relatively quickly from both recurrent crop failures and the sort of "extreme event" (Johnson, 1973, *loc. cit.*) which I describe later.

Equally important is the fact that the Mursi live in an environment which is climatically marginal. What little metereological information that exists for the lower Omo region (none of it, unfortunately, coming from Mursi country itself) has been carefully collated by Butzer (1971), and it is on his account that I base my estimate that maximum mean annual rainfall in Mursi country is around 500 mm. The minimum rainfall necessary for regular reliable cropping is usually estimated at 700 mm. a year (Brown, 1973, p. 68), areas with less than this annual mean being unable to support a purely agricultural way of life. It is not so much the quantity of rain, measured as an annual mean, which is important, however, as the fact that, in these arid and semi-arid areas of Africa rainfall is extremely variable, both as to timing and locality. More important than quantity, then, is the probability of enough rain falling in any one year or growing season to make successful cultivation possible. I have no figures with which to demonstrate this variability for Mursi country, but a failure of the rains over part or all of the country once every two or three years seemed to be expected, nor was a failure for two consecutive years unheard of. What was unheard of, in living memory, until 1973, was a failure of the rains for three consecutive years.

Most of the rain which falls in Mursi country is concentrated into two periods of two to three weeks, one in March/April, the primary maximum, and the other in October/November. The period spanning these two rainfall maxima may be regarded as the wet season. There are occasional showers during this time, while water can be obtained fairly easily along several stretches of the Omo's westward flowing tributaries. Apart from the Omo itself, water is most easily available from the streams which flow down the north-western slopes of the Mursi Mountains, none of which, however, flows for more than a few days after rain has fallen. At the height of the dry season, in December and January, even these sources of water may dry up.

The Omo, however, is a permanent river, most of the catchment area of which lies above 1000 m (Butzer, 1971, p. 3), with the result that it is affected more by the rainfall which falls over the Ethiopian highlands (1500–2500 m) than by that which falls over its lower basin. By April or May the river begins to rise, and reaches its maximum level in August, when it deposits layers of flood silt along its banks. More extensive flooding occurs on the gently inclined slip-off slopes on the inner bends of meanders, but, for most of its course in Mursi country (north of latitude 5.30 N.) the Omo does not meander markedly, so that the area flooded is never as large as it is further south, in the delta plain. Having reached its maximum level, the Omo recedes rapidly in September and October, and is easily fordable, at several places, by December. During the wet season it may be crossed by dugout canoe, but, between May and September, the speed and turbulence of the current makes this a dangerous undertaking.

I have heard the lower Omo valley described, by people enthusiastic for wildlife conservation, as "one of the last wildernesses of Africa", which should be preserved in its "original" state. In a sense, however, it is no more of a wilderness than the lower Thames valley—it "wears man's smudge" even if it is not "seared with trade" (G. M. Hopkins, *God's Grandeur*). Flanking the Omo on the eastern, Mursi side, to an average depth of about 6 km is a belt of bushland thicket, that is, "an extreme form" of bushland "where the woody plants form a closed stand through which man or the larger ungulates can pass only with extreme difficulty and in which the land has no value for grazing" (Pratt, *et al.*, 1966, p. 373). This bushbelt, wherein are found such plants as *Sarcostemma, Euphorbia tirucali, Cissus quadrangularis, Sanseviera, Acacia mellifera, Adenium obesum* and *Plectranthus*, has probably been created by a combination of overgrazing and shifting cultivation. It not only provides no grazing, but also harbours the tsetse fly, and is therefore doubly inhospitable to cattle. The bushbelt gives way abruptly, however, to open wooded grassland which rises steadily towards the Omo-Mako watershed, and which provides good grazing. Here are found, scattered or in groups, such trees as *Commiphora africana*, *Commiphora pendunculata*, *Combretum fragrans*, *Sclerocarya*, *Lannea* and *Grewia villosa*. South and west of the Mursi Mountains, where the climate appears to be more arid than in the rest of the country, the rapidly drained sandy soil supports only dwarf shrub grassland (Fig. 2).

The Mursi are able to survive in this isolated and marginal environment because their means of subsistence are relatively diverse and complementary, because their social organisation is adapted to the equitable distribution of resources and to the spreading of risk, and because the human and animal populations are subject to implacable "natural" checks.

Diversification of Subsistence

The Mursi's chief means of subsistence are (1) cattle[2] herding in the grass plain, (2) shifting cultivation in the bushbelt, and (3) flood-retreat[3] cultivation along the banks of the Omo. Each one of these is insufficient and precarious in itself but, when taken together with the other two, makes a vital contribution to subsistence.

Pastoral activities are confined to the area designated on fig. 2 as wooded grassland, since only here can the three basic requirements of cattle for water, grazing and at least relative freedom from disease, be met. Apart from being infested with tsetse flies, the bushbelt contains only isolated and minute patches of open grassland, mainly on sandy cliffs close to the Omo. Cattle are, however, taken to the Omo for short periods almost every year, either because of shortage of water in the plain and/or because of attacks, or the threat of attacks, from neighbouring groups. This movement of cattle to the Omo usually takes place in January or December, the height of the

[2] The Mursi keep a few goats and fewer sheep, but small stock are a relatively insignificant part of their economy.

[3] I use this rather cumbersome term to indicate that the flood recedes rapidly, after a matter of days, cultivation then taking place on the land which it has inundated.

dry season, when water is scarce in the eastern plain, when the Mako is easily fordable by prospective cattle raiders, and when the Omo crop is ready to be harvested. In general, however, the Omo is a place to which cattle may be taken for short periods, under pressure, but not one at which they can safely remain for any length of time.

It has been estimated that two or three "Standard Stock Units" per head of population is the minimum required to provide adequately for daily subsistence in a purely pastoral economy, where one Standard Stock Unit equals 454 kg—or about two adult cattle of the type generally found among East African herders (Brown, 1973, p. 69). At the time I visited them, the Mursi had no more than one adult animal—or, in other words, half a Standard Stock Unit—per head of population, which would mean, if the above calculation is correct, that they had no more than a quarter of the cattle they would have needed in order to survive entirely on a diet of milk, blood and meat. They can thus only be called pastoralists in a subjective sense— they maintain the values and outlook of a pastoral people, despite the fact that cultivation provides a greater proportion of their subsistence needs than does pastoralism. Their herds are, however, of the greatest importance in maintaining the viability of their total economy for, as will be seen shortly, and as is already partly apparent from what has been said about rainfall, cultivation, whether of the shifting or flood-retreat kind, cannot be relied upon to provide an adequate and regular food supply. Cattle can be moved around to take maximum advantage of available grazing and water, thus neutralizing, to some extent, the variability of the rainfall. They therefore provide something to fall back on in the event of crop failure or a poor harvest, while in extreme conditions they can be exchanged for grain, both within and beyond Mursi country. The Mursi themselves express this complementarity by saying that "cattle and grain are one".

Although rainfall in Mursi country is sparse and variable, if there is a sufficiently heavy fall of rain in March or early April, sorghum, planted in the newly moistened black soil of the bushbelt, will ripen in ten weeks and be ready for harvesting in 12. A little maize which is more sensitive than sorghum to drought, since it has a longer growing season (Baker, 1974, p. 175), is also planted in the bushbelt, following the March/April rain. If the rain is late, however, falling in late April or early May, even sorghum will not have enough time to reach maturity, before it is destroyed by the sun. Rainfall is the only limiting factor in bushbelt cultivation, there being no shortage of land. The dilemma is that the bush has to be burned off before the end of the dry season and thus before it is known whether there will be enough rain to make successful cultivation of the prepared plots possible. It should be added that it is also possible to have too much rain: seeds may be washed out of the ground, and weeds and pests encouraged.

Sorghum is also the main crop at the Omo, where it is planted, together with maize, beans and cow peas, as the river recedes in September. Since no form of irrigation is practiced, only land which has actually been inundated by the flood can be cultivated. The topography of the banks thus sets a physical limit to the amount of cultivable land. On the other hand, and in contrast to bushbelt cultivation, preparations for planting (clearing away river-bank vegetation which has grown up over the wet season) can be limited to land which is known to be cultivable, because it has already been flooded. Since flood-retreat cultivation is not subject to the vicissitudes of the local rainfall, it is a vital link in the Mursi's subsistence chain. The land flooded in any one year, however, is not extensive. This is a valuable, though limited resource, which is consequently allocated according to more strict rules than either grazing land—to which there is open and egalitarian access—or bushbelt land for shifting cultivation. If a man is asked how he came to be cultivating at a particular spot in the bushbelt, he may reply that his father cultivated thereabouts before him, or that he had been allocated a plot which had already been cleared, probably by a kinsman of his wife, or he may say "I just cleared it—it was bush here before". Where Omo cultivation is concerned, however, the same question will receive either the first or the second answer, but never the third—one never goes and "just clears' a plot at the Omo.

The problem of Mursi subsistence may be described as that of spanning these geographically separate natural resources with the human ones necessary to exploit them successfully. In solving this problem they have developed a form of transhumance which, although it takes place over a relatively small area, does not permit fixed residence in a single locality by an section of the population. Between April and September, when water can be obtained from holes dug in the beds of the Omo's westward flowing tributaries, cattle settlements are established around the headstreams of these tributaries, and within a short distance of the bushbelt cultivation areas. During these months the population is relatively concentrated, but the settlements, which consist of beehive huts of grass in thorn and brush-wood compounds, are by no means permanent, either from one year to the next or during a single season. In September and October the women, girls and young children move to the Omo to begin planting while the men and boys take the cattle eastward in search of water and grazing. These two sections of the population do not converge again until March/April, when new cattle settlements are constructed in the vicinity of the bushbelt. Thus, the transhumance movements of the Mursi may be thought of as a process of dispersal from (in September/October) and convergence on (in March/April) an area from which, for part of the year, both pastoral and agricultural activities can be carried on, but which can support neither of them, because of lack of water, for the rest of the year. This central zone represents the meeting of what might be called the "two worlds" of the Mursi—that of the Omo, the world of cultivation, of women and of relative ease and security, and that of the eastern plain, the world of cattle, of men, and of relative hardship and danger. The subsistence problems of the Mursi therefore lead to a degree of mobility which, at first sight, is surprising in a population which occupies, effectively, a territory measuring no more than 55 kilometres by 28.

The three chief means of subsistence which I have described here are, at the best of times, in a relatively delicate balance. It should be noted also that, although some storage of grain takes place, the amount stored by any particular family is, at most, barely sufficient to be eked out till the next harvest. One factor which prevents the storage of large quantities of grain is that, since there are no permanent settlements, grain stores could not be guarded against animal or human predation. Other factors are insect pests and humidity, with neither of which can the Mursi deal satisfactorily, given their existing technology. As it is, grain is stored in spherical containers, made of thin branches and covered with grass, which vary in diameter from 50 to 80 cm and which each family hides in the bushbelt, in the branches of trees. Even if these containers are not broken into by baboons (a frequent occurrence), their contents may well be damaged by heavy rain.

The Mursi also engage in hunting, especially of the buffalo, their weapon being the 8 mm Mannlicher rifle, which was carried by the Italian troops who occupied Ethiopia between 1936 and 1941. They obtain these rifles, and ammunition, from highland traders, in exchange for leopard skins, ivory and cattle. Fishing takes place at the Omo in the dry season, it being an important standby in the weeks before the Omo crop is harvested. Two methods of fishing are employed: boys use lines and baited hooks thrown into the water from a shingle beach or bar, while adult men stalk fish singly, with harpoons, standing in shallow water near the bank. Certain berries and roots are also utilized as "famine foods", although children will eat them "for fun" in normal times. With these means of subsistence to fall back on and with, at the best of times, a delicately balanced economy, the Mursi think of themselves as being innured to hunger. It is something they know about, and with which they have learned to cope. When I was first with them they told me that, although they were often hungry, there was never any question of anyone dying of hunger. By 1973 they were unable to make such a claim.

Social Organization

The unit of production and consumption in Mursi society is, ideally, a family group consisting of a man, his wives and their unmarried children. In practice, however, such a unit cannot maintain strict economic independence, both because of the need to span geographically distinct pastoral and agricultural resources, and also because of the special requirements of herding. Thus, it may be necessary for a man to absent himself frequently from his cattle in order to help with his wife with agricultural tasks—not only clearing and planting, but also bird-scaring—and at such times he may need to rely on another herd owner to look after his cattle. Economic co-operation between the members of a cattle settlement—a survey I carried out in 1970 revealed an average of seven married men per settlement—is essential in order to allow as many individuals as possible to keep a foothold in each of the two "worlds" I have just described. The labour requirements of herding call for a boy of about eight to look after the calves close by the settlement, a boy of about 14 to take the cattle to their daily grazing, and an older boy to take charge of the herd in the absence of the herd owner. The separate compounds of a cattle settlement thus represent only an ideal autonomy of individual family heads. The cattle of each compound are not herded separately, common decisions as to grazing movements and watering being made by means of discussion among the individual herd owners of the settlement.

Although the Mursi think of their society as being divided into cohesive groups on the basis of descent through males, this patrilineal ideology is not significant in determining patterns of economic co-operation and local residence. The survey of cattle settlements just mentioned revealed that by far the most common ties linking the married men of a cattle settlement were affinal ones—putting it crudely, men tended to live and co-operate on a day to day basis with their brothers-in-law rather than with their own brothers. The significance of this pattern lies in the high degree of residential mobility which also characterizes Mursi settlements, this mobility being itself a concomittant of uncertain and fluctuating ecological conditions. Cattle settlements are impermanent, not only in relation to their physical structures and locations, but also in relation to their inhabitants: people who are found living together for anything from three to six months during one wet season may well be living apart during the next. Such flexibility is necessary in order to ensure the equitable distribution of available resources, both human and material, and it is achieved by the utilization of a wide variety of interpersonal kinship and affinal ties.

In view of the importance of affinity, and of the symbolic and economic role of cattle in Mursi society, it is appropriate to consider here the way in which bridewealth cattle are distributed, this being, incidentally, the most important economic transaction in which any Mursi is likely to be involved. An examination of this subject reveals that, although the payment of bridewealth is not an economic transaction of the type with which we, from our market-oriented viewpoint, are familiar, it does, nevertheless, have a lot to do, if not with short-term enrichment, then with long-term security.

Eight different families, including that of the bride herself, and corresponding to her eight great grandparents, are involved in the distribution of a girl's bridewealth. This should consist, ideally, of 38 cattle, but, in my experience, rarely totals more than 24. Apart from the cattle "eaten" by the bride's father and/or brothers, ten should go to the bride's mother's brother (MB) or, if he is dead, to

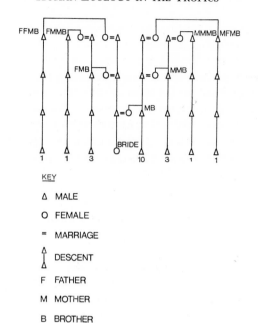

KEY

Δ MALE

O FEMALE

= MARRIAGE

⬆ DESCENT

F FATHER

M MOTHER

B BROTHER

NUMBERS REFER TO HEAD OF CATTLE

FIG. 3. The distribution of bridewealth among relatives of the bride, outside her own nuclear family.

her mother's brother's son. Three should go to the descendants of her paternal grandmother's brother (MMB), and three to the descendants of her paternal grandmother's brother (FMB). One should go to the descendants of her mother's maternal grandmother's brother (MMMB), one to the descendants of her mother's paternal grandmother's brother (MFMB), one to the descendants of her father's maternal grandmother's brother (FMMB), and one to the descendants of her father's paternal grandmother's brother (FFMB). Such a transaction therefore has what might be called a time depth of three generations—it is complex not only because of the number of families which are involved, but also because of the number of previous marriages to which it is connected. For each marriage looks back ideally, to seven previous marriages—those of the bride's parents, grandparents and great grandparents—and the distribution of bridewealth may be looked upon as a series of "deferred payments" (Evans-Pritchard, 1951, p. 78) for these marriages. Thus, for example, the payment made to the bride's father's mother's brother (or his descendants) may be seen as an instalment of bridewealth for the marriage of her paternal grandmother to her paternal grandfather. Finally, it is this distribution of cattle to families other than that of the bride herself which, more than the simple acquisition of cattle by her own family, establishes the legality of the marriage. If any of the people designated above feel that they have not been properly considered they can put a curse on the new marriage which will make it infertile, or cause any children born to it to die. Such children are said to die from a disease, the principal symptom of which is constant salivation, whence the fact that these relatives of the bride, who have a right to share in her bridewealth but who are not members of her own family, are called "people of the saliva".

I have described, very briefly, a valuable and complex transaction which is supported by powerful sanctions. There is clearly more to it than the short term economic gain of those to whom the bridewealth is initially handed over—the bride's family. For, as Glickman has put it, writing of the Nuer, "bridewealth is not necessarily paid to the bride's father, but distributed among a number of homesteads in payment of debts that the bride's father has contracted" (1971, p. 314). If one looks at long term security, however, rather than at short term enrichment, this distribution is not without economic advantage. In the first place, it helps to create and maintain a wide network of ties, giving any particular individual involved a number of possibilities for pressing claims in the future, not necessarily for cattle, but for any resource of which he is in need at a particular time. In the second place, any man who distributes a daughter's or a sister's bridewealth will have been and/or will be in the future on the receiving end of other such distributions. If it is objected that, in a purely economic sense, there would, logically, be no net gain or loss for any individual as a result of these transactions, the answer is twofold. On the one hand, it should be noted that it is not the economic but the moral component of these exchanges which enables them to create the network of ties just mentioned. This kind of exchange is not *essentially* economic, but is what Mauss has called a "total social phenomenon" (1954, p. 1)—an event which is, at the same time, social, religious, moral and utilitarian. On the other hand, it is clearly economically rational to distribute one's animals widely in an environment where they are at risk from such arbitrary dangers as disease, raiders and wild animals. In doing so one is giving up the immediate ownership of an asset in exchange for a promise of future return—one does not, of course, expect to receive back the same animal, any more than one would expect to receive back from a bank the same notes that one deposited.

Bridewealth distribution, then, is neither a purely economic transaction, nor is it a "futile drama" (Levi–Strauss, 1969, p. 60). It is the most important factor in the creation of a network of ties which allow, in turn, for residential mobility and for flexibility in relations of economic co-operation. It is, furthermore, a means of sharing wealth, of spreading risk and of hedging against future shortage.

Population Control

The third factor that must be taken into account in any discussion of the survival of the Mursi in a marginal and isolated environment is the control of animal and human numbers.

The Mursi are expert cattle herders, and their social organisation is such that the needs of the cattle are given priority over almost every other consideration. Thus, there is always a category of young, unmarried men available to move with the cattle to where the grazing and water is most plentiful and to defend them from raiders by means of scouting expeditions and pre-emptive or retaliatory attacks. Their cattle usually look, admittedly to an untrained eye, in excellent condition, even during the dry season. Since they keep cattle principally for their milk, and since they therefore aim to maximize the proportion of female animals in their herds, these have a very rapid potential rate of increase—in favourable conditions perhaps somewhere between 4% and 10% per annum (Allan, 1965, p. 316). The picture that emerges from other parts of East Africa, where pastoralists have had the "advantage" of veterinary services, is of a rapid build-up of stock numbers in favourable years and then a drastic reduction in numbers due to cyclic drought, but not before widespread damage has been done to the environment by over-grazing. For the Mursi, who have, as yet, no access to veterinary services, it is not drought but disease which controls this process of growth.

Bovine trypanosomiasis takes a constant toll, since the tsetse fly is now found not only in the bushbelt, but also in the eastern plain.

Middle-aged men say that they have "grown up with" the fly—that it has, in other words, gradually spread during their lifetime. It is likely that the tsetse was present in the riverine forest along the Omo before the present bushbelt developed. The fly in question was probably *Glossina fuscipes* which, since it is not a good vector of bovine trypanosomiasis, would not have seriously interfered with the keeping of cattle along the Omo.   The creation of the bushbelt—largely, it is suggested, through overgrazing—probably allowed entry to *Glossina pallidipes*, a thicket tsetse which is a good vector of the bovine disease[4].

More dramatic, and more feared than the losses due to tsetse fly, however, are those which result from rinderpest. Four epidemics have occurred in Mursi country since 1947, at intervals of approximately seven years. Because of this seven year pattern they were expecting another outbreak in 1974, but this had not occurred by the time we left them, in August of that year[5]. Their pessimism was deepened by the very heavy rains of the 1974 wet season, for it seems that there is also an association between very wet conditions and rinderpest. This periodicity of the disease is presumably related to the number of years it takes to build up a new body of non-immune and therefore endangered stock, and the association with wet conditions to the fact that these favour the survival of the virus, which "does not live for more than 24 hours away from the animal's body in tropical sunshine, but in damp and shade may remain infective for a week or more" (Mackenzie and Simpson, 1971, p. 66)[6]. According to Mackenzie and Simpson (*loc. cit*) about 50% of sick animals die during an epidemic, the remaining 50% recovering completely and being immune for the rest of their lives.

The human population is subject to such epidemic diseases as cholera, smallpox and measles, the latter having, it would seem, a high fatality among young children. Although there are no infant mortality figures to go on, it can be assumed that, if these existed for the Mursi, they would show a rate of around 50%. It can also

[4] I am grateful to W. P. Langridge for a conversation which led to these suggestions.
[5] I was told, however, by Dr. Ivo Strecker, that the Hamar had come across buffalo, dead from rinderpest, in the Mako valley in May.
[6] I am grateful to Dr. P. T. W. Baxter for drawing my attention to this reference.

be assumed that, in times of hardship, an increased mortality rate would show itself mainly among that section of the population which has the highest rate at the best of times—namely, young children (Seaman, *et al.*, 1974, pp. 41–42). In normal times, therefore, those reaching maturity will represent the survivors of a fairly drastic process of selection, and it is to be expected that the survival rate among adults, especially young adults, will be relatively high. This is born out by Table 1, in which, together with Tables 2 and 3, I have presented information relating to mortality over a four year period among married men who were part of a census I carried out in 1969–70.

The absence of outside administrative influence also shows itself in the incidence of death by homicide, especially the killing of Mursi by non-Mursi. It can be seen from Table 2 that homicide was the next most important cause of death after "illness" in the 30–40 age group, and in the sample as a whole. From Table 3 it can be seen that out of 14 cases of homicide recorded, 12 were the result of the

TABLE 1. SURVIVAL RATE OF MARRIED MEN BETWEEN 1970 and 1974

Estimated age range, 1970	Recorded alive, 1970	Recorded alive, 1974	Survival rate, over 4 years
			%
30–40	201	172	86
40–50	78	57	73
50–60	56	47	84
60–70	28	21	75
70+	4	1	25
	367	298	81

TABLE 2. CAUSE OF DEATH AS A PERCENTAGE OF ALL DEATHS IN EACH AGE GROUP

Estimated age range, 1970	Illness		Hunger		Accident		Homicide	
	%		%		%		%	
30–40	59	(17)	—		7	(2)	34	(10)
40–50	57	(12)	14	(3)	14	(3)	14	(3)
50–60	56	(5)	33	(3)	—		11	(1)
60–70	57	(4)	43	(3)	—		—	
70+	67	(2)	33	(1)				
All dead	58	(40)	14	(10)	7	(5)	20	(14)

TABLE 3. BREAKDOWN OF CAUSES OF DEATH IN TABLE 2

Estimated Age Range 1970	ILLNESS			HUNGER		ACCIDENT		HOMICIDE		TOTAL
	Smallpox	Cholera	Other	Starvation	Suicide	Hunting	Other	Mursi	Non-Mursi	Total
30-40	3	7	7	–	–	2	–	1	9	29
40-50	–	6	6	3	–	–	3	1	2	21
50-60	1	1	3	3	–	–	–	–	1	9
60-70	–	–	4	2	1	–	–	–	–	7
70+	–	–	2	–	1	–	–	–	–	3
Total and as % all dead	4 (6%)	14 (20%)	22 (32%)	8 (12%)	2 (3%)	2 (3%)	3 (4%)	2 (3%)	12 (17%)	69 (100%)

killing of Mursi by non-Mursi. I am not suggesting that these figures are typical, since this four-year period was one of extreme hardship for the Mursi, but they are probably fairly reliable as a guide to the relative significance of the different causes of death in the age groups concerned.

Another important consideration here is the incidence of abandonment. This is not a subject which figures much in existing accounts of such groups as the Mursi, mainly, perhaps, because it is not something which the people themselves like to talk about. The fact is, however, that, among the Mursi, any individual who is immobile —or who is mentally defective to a degree that makes him unable to carry on the activities appropriate to his age group—will, sooner or later, be abandoned by his family. This would apply, for example, to a four year old child who had suffered brain damage after being bitten by a poisonous spider, to a teenage boy with polio, to a young man wounded badly in the thigh during a cattle raid by a neighbouring group, or to an old man who had become blind. Children who are born defective are allowed to live if it is thought possible that they will achieve normality. Otherwise they are suffocated. Although a person may be carried by his relatives from wet season to dry season areas of settlement for two or three years, there will eventually come a time when he will be left in the bush to die. Such a fate may well be hastened by periods of crisis, such as famine and war, but it must be stressed that the practice of abandonment is not a response to unusually harsh conditions. It is rather a fact of every-day life for the Mursi. It follows, principally, from the fact that there are no areas of permanent settlement, and from the fact that the Mursi do not make use of pack animals. The consequences of losing physical mobility is a theme which crops up frequently in the myths and legends told by the Mursi. These include stories of a man who became so fat that he could no longer walk and therefore had to be left behind when his sons moved their settlement, and of a girl who was born with no legs.

The Mursi are committed to growth, both in animal and human numbers, but, given their technology and environment, this ideology is necessary in order to maintain those numbers and does not, by itself, promise ecological doom. If medical and veterinary services were introduced, of course, and warfare were controlled, the commitment of the people to animal and human population growth would lead to a drastic upsetting of the ecological balance and to an equally drastic, periodic, restoring of that balance. It seems clear that the dramatic stock losses reported in times of "drought" from various parts of Africa—1 500 000 head of cattle, for example, in the Sukuma district of Tanzania in 1949—have been as much the result of overstocking, following the introduction of veterinary services, the boring of wells and increases in human population, as of water shortage (Baker, 1974, p. 174; Brown, 1973, p. 72). In a sense, therefore, and as Spencer (1974) points out, "drought" has been created by a process of economic and technological growth to which we in our society are as committed as the pastoralists are to demographic growth and to the growth of their herds.

The Drought of 1971 to 1973

Between 1971 and 1973 the Mursi experienced what was agreed to be the worst food shortage that anyone could remember, and it was caused by an equally unprecedented failure of the rain—for three consecutive years. These were also years of poor rainfall over the Ethiopian plateau, with the result that the Omo flood was a poor one in 1971 and 1972. Nor were fish plentiful in the Omo during this period. In 1971 the Mursi were affected by cholera, and in the following year by smallpox—though deaths from the latter disease were far fewer than from the former (see Table 3). Towards the end of 1971 their relations with the neighbouring Bodi, which had been under strain for some time, broke down into all-out war, which was continuing when we were last in the area, in August 1974. In September 1973 the Mursi received a distribution of famine relief from the Ethiopian Government, the grain being flown to a landing strip about 65 km north of the Mara, in Bodi country. In December 1973, through the efforts of the British Embassy, Oxfam and Christian Aid, they received a further 3000 kg of grain, which was flown by the Ethiopian Airforce to the same landing strip. (Although they were escorted by police for part of these journeys into Bodi country, one Mursi was shot dead by a Bodi a few minutes walk from the landing strip.) There was a good flood in 1973, and in January and February 1974 a good harvest was obtained at the Omo. In April 1974 there was exceptionally heavy rain in Mursi country, although the subsequent, July, harvest was badly affected by insect pests.

N I

How serious was this period of hardship for the Mursi? By their own account it was disastrous, but is it possible to apply any objective measure? One way to attempt this would be to consider the death rate for the period, and this can be done, at least for a section of the population, because I was able to replicate, in 1973–74, the census of married men which I had carried out in 1969–70. It can be seen from Table 2 that the biggest single cause of death was "illness", though this included cholera which, from Table 3, can be seen to have accounted for 20% of all deaths within this section of the population.

In this latter table I have attributed to "starvation" those deaths which were so attributed by the Mursi, or in accounting for which they emphasized hunger. Two of the deaths recorded here were the result of suicide—in both cases, old men who had become an evident burden on their families. One went off to the bush to die, and the other drowned himself in the Omo. It is of course extremely difficult accurately to estimate the indirect significance of food shortage in these figures, especially where "other" illness is concerned. One death which I have classified as an accident was said to have been the result of over-eating—the man in question gorged himself on fish and porridge after a period of near starvation. One of the "hunting accidents" came about when a man who was searching for honey in a rocky place became wedged in a cleft of the rock, lost his foothold and could not free himself. A boy he was with gave the alarm, but the man's relatives were too weak from hunger to attempt—or to be prepared to attempt—the 20 mile walk to save his life.

Despite such facts, however, it is impossible to come to quantifiable conclusions about the seriousness of this period of hardship for the Mursi. In the first place, with figures for this period only, it is impossible to show that there was anything unusual, either about the overall death rate or about the different causes of death. In the second place, that section of the population which can be assumed to have the highest mortality rate at the best of times and which it can also be assumed will have an even higher mortality rate in times of hardship—children under 15—is excluded from these figures. The authors of a recent report on drought in Harerghe Province, south-east Ethiopia (Seaman et al., 1974), found that it was the young children of the pastoral populations of the area who suffered the greatest increase in mortality over a year of drought[7]. The same authors also noted a reduced birth rate and comment that this phenomenon has been found elsewhere "in times of severe hardship" (p. 43). Thus, as far as the adult population is concerned, one would not expect the effects of a period of extreme food shortage to show up, in a society which is, at the best of times, delicately balanced against the natural environment, until about 20 years after the crisis has passed.

It may be more sensible, therefore, to estimate the seriousness of a period of hardship in a subjective way—to look at the response of the people, rather than to attempt an objective measure. This would require, first of all, that one listen to what the people themselves say about it. Secondly, one would have to look at the various measures they adopted to overcome the problem, and thirdly, one would have to ask whether these measures put an unusual strain on social relations. For, if one assumes that a particular social organization is, at least partly, an adaptation to a particular system of exploiting the environment, it is likely that, if that system of exploitation goes seriously awry, some effects will be evident on social relations.

The 1971–73 food shortage was the worst the Mursi could remember. What did they do about it? In general, they employed the procedures which they were used to employing to cope with recurrent shortage, only to a greater extent. As was noted above, and unlike the Tigrean peasants who were so badly hit by drought in the north of Ethiopia during the same period, the Mursi are, as they say, used to hunger: they expect it and have conventional procedures for coping with it. Famine foods are utilized, while hunting, fishing and honey gathering are, where possible, intensified. Cattle are bled more frequently and cattle raids are launched against neighbouring groups. But, according to the Mursi, the single most important factor in enabling them to survive during these years was the sale of cattle for grain in the highlands. They were clear that it was the cattle that had saved them, and that it had been those with no cattle to exchange for grain who had been the hardest hit. Although this was the worst

---

[7] cf. also Firth's account of Tikopia in Famine: "For about three months the death rate on the island rose to three or two persons a week, or to about four times its normal level. Those most affected were the very old, and especially the very young, who were the least able to fend for themselves, in foraging for food scraps" (1959, p. 62).

N 2

period of hunger in living memory, it was compared to an earlier period, known as *rokobo*, and which probably occurred in the last decade of the nineteenth century. I was told that *rokobo* had been even worse, because at that time they had no cattle to exchange for grain. There was widespread rinderpest in East Africa in the 1890's, which seems to have been a disastrous decade altogether (Allan, 1965, p. 317), and when the Italian explorer, Bottego, followed the left bank of the Omo through Musi country in 1896, he reported that the Mursi were living mainly by hunting and fishing.

It is already clear from what I have said about bridewealth distribution that a cow is not just a market object for the Mursi. It is not only the single most prized economic possession, it is also a focus of social relations, carrying, in other words, a moral component. It is by bearing this in mind that the true significance for the Mursi of parting with a stock animal for a few weeks or even a few days supply of grain, can be appreciated. Other objects bartered for grain were rifles (worth four head of cattle in Mursi country), skins (of cattle and buffalo), tobacco, and honey. This trade clearly involved more than usual movement by the Mursi into the highlands —indeed, one effect of this period of shortage has undoubtedly been increased contact between the Mursi and the "outside world". A few people obtained cultivation rights from particular friends among the agriculturalists on the lower slopes of the highlands to the east of the Omo, and they appeared to have moved there permanently. Several people left children with traders and police to be taken back when the crisis was over. In 1972 and 1973 large numbers of Mursi went into Jinka, where they were able to earn a little money and/or food by carrying wood and water for the local people. They also raided the honey barrels of the people living in and around Jinka, and then proceeded to sell the honey in Jinka market.

Such behaviour naturally did not add to their popularity in Jinka and surrounding areas where, at the best of times, they are regarded with that mixture of fear and contempt which sedentary agriculturalists commonly reserve for their pastoral neighbours. There were many deaths as a result of this coming and going of the Mursi to the highlands. One night, for example, eight of them were speared and killed as they slept in Jinka market-place, after which a special hut was built for Mursi to sleep in, at the air-strip. People were also killed on the way to and from both Jinka and another highland settlement to the north-west of Jinka, which the Mursi call Dauwi. There were seven deaths on this latter route, due to Bodi snipers, over two years. The fact that people were prepared, not only to part with such highly prized possessions as cattle and rifles, but also to undertake these dangerous journeys into the highlands is a sufficient indication of the seriousness of the food shortage experienced by the Mursi during these years. None of the measures they adopted, however, were, in themselves, new or unusual to them. What was unusual was the scale on which they were put into practice, a scale which caused a great deal of adverse comment from speakers in public meetings, when the worst of the hardship was over:

"We Mursi have always known what it is like to be hungry, and yet people did not go on journeys to get grain before. They would stay here, hungry, their skin hanging loose round their buttocks, eating leaves, bleeding a single cow, first on one side and then on the other, so that it would have large scars on both sides of its neck. Where did this idea of going to get grain come from? Did it come from outside, or did it originate here?"

"Hunger is something one just has to put up with: one just binds one's stomach tightly and waits till it passes."

Comments like these contained the implication that large scale turning away from "traditional" behaviour was not so much the result as the cause of the crisis. I wrote above that it was to be expected that the effects of severe economic hardship would be observable in the conduct of social relations. The Mursi too see a connection here, but they do not see it in quite the same light. For them, disruption of the natural order is caused by disruption of the social order. Natural disasters, such as drought, disease and war result, according to this view, from the failure of individuals to observe the traditional values of Mursi society. The speakers who made the above comments were saying, in a sense quite rightly, that if people had concentrated their efforts on eking out an existence at home, taking care to plant what seed they had at the right time— in short, if they had behaved traditionally—they would not have been killed in the highlands, and on journeys to get grain. It is believed that, if only people would accept traditional values in their everyday lives, then material prosperity would be assured, and this is true, to the extent that the observance of, for example, kinship and affinal obligations contribute to the survival of the group in a marginal environment.

But an "extreme" event is precisely one which the group affected cannot take in its stride, on the basis of traditional norms. It is to be expected that conventions of, for example, sharing, hospitality and generosity will go by the board in times of extreme scarcity, when individual survival becomes the prime concern. Failure to observe these conventions can, of course, be seen by the people as a break-down of social order causing, rather than resulting from, the disaster. Such a situation has been described by Firth in his study of Tikopia in a time of famine (1959, Chapters III and IV). He found that stealing became an acute problem, that land disputes increased in number, that quarrels between brothers and close agnates holding land in common were frequent and that there was an "increased limitation on communal rights in food". He also notes that there was a widespread belief that the crisis was man-made—in particular that it was created by, and not the cause of, widespread stealing—and comments that it was a "socially healthy attitude to lay the blame on the human factor and not on the vagaries of nature". Despite what he calls "some atomization of the wider kin groups", however, Firth found that "sharing within the elementary family continued to be the norm, even at the height of the famine" (p. 83), and that "Men and women were concerned not merely for themselves, but especially for their children " (p. 64).

A more recent study of the social effects of extreme food shortage —that by Turnbull of a settled, but once nomadic group of hunters in northern Uganda, the Ik—presents a picture of individualism "cultivated . . . to its apex" (1972, p. 284). According to Turnbull, the Ik were not only "dehumanized" while the famine lasted, but were, by the time it had passed, finished "as a society". The experi-ence of trying to do fieldwork at such a time was clearly a harrowing one, and it may well be that Turnbull's account reflects, intentionally or not, the influence of the fieldwork experience on him, rather than the impact of the famine on the Ik. It is, in any event, worth keeping in mind, or when reading such an account, the potentially "dehumani-zing" experience that people in all societies, including, presumably, that of the Ik, learn to live with and to accept, however reluctantly, as the price of valued forms of adaption. For the Mursi, such an experience is the abandoning of the incapacitated, the price of movement, while in our society, one of our most valued mechanisms of adaptation, the motor car, is also the most lethal.

I have an opposite problem to that of Turnbull in trying to estimate the effects of the 1971–73 drought on social relations among the Mursi. For whereas he was with the Ik during the worst of the famine, but could not compare what he saw with "normal" conditions, I do not have first hand experience of the Mursi's response to their period of hardship. I was, however, given accounts, such as that of the man trapped in a rock cleft, which resembled some of the incidents which Turnbull records as evidence of the "dehumanization of the Ik. According to Mursi sentiment, there is no stronger tie than that between full brothers, and yet this man's two full brothers did not attempt to save him. The reason given for this was that they were too weak from hunger to make the journey—that they preferred to conserve their energy at a time when some people were starving to death. A closer examination of this case, however, revealed other factors which were admitted by the Mursi to have contributed to the failure of the man's brothers to save him. He had no cattle, and although he had two sons, the oldest of these, who had accompanied him on the honey gathering expedition, was only about 12. He was also a widower, and I was told that, had his wife been alive, she could have put pressure on his brothers by threatening that she would not agree to being inherited by them if her husband died as a result of their failure to rescue him. In other words, the man was poor and without advocates, and it must be admitted that, even in "normal" times, this is a parlous position in which to find oneself.

A more significant indication of strain in social relations is the fact that there was, apparently, a marked increase in the rate at which disputes between individuals were brought into the public arena. Among the Mursi, a fairly elaborate procedure is involved in public dispute settlement, which involves the disputants duelling with poles, six feet long. They are restrained by a crowd of neutral onlookers to allow the intervention of one or more "referees", or mediators (Turton, 1973). During my first visit to the Mursi I witnessed only two such events in the 18 months I spent among them. It seems, therefore, that disagreements and conflicts between individuals are only rarely of such an intractable kind that they have to be brought to such a public settlement. During this period of hunger, however, people began calling in debts and pressing claims which, in less difficult times, they might have left dormant. Particularly significant here is the fact that there was even a tendency for cattle which had been paid in bridewealth to be recalled—or rather, taken back by force. It was as though it was no longer possible to wait for reciprocity to be achieved in its own time. The Mursi had lost confidence in the natural order of things and they had, so to speak, lost confidence in their social order as well. They therefore began turning their long term, intangible assets—claims on the property of others based on kinship, affinity and past exchanges—into short term, tangible ones. Indeed, several people told me, before the rain fell in 1974, that they thought it had deserted Mursi country for good, and that their only hope was to do the same—to migrate to the highlands.

As they emerged from the worst of the crisis the Mursi were in what could be called a state of shock, which is hardly surprising in view of what I have just written. They were also by no means certain what the future held, firstly because the war with the Bodi was continuing to cause serious problems for them in the management of their herds, and secondly because they were confidently expecting a rinderpest epidemic. But there was no evidence of a permanent breakdown of their social and economic organization, such as Turnbull reports for the Ik. The physical recovery of the population—given, of course, that many peeple did not survive at all—also seemed to be rapid. In June and July 1974 my wife carried out a weight for height survey of 106 children between the ages of 3 and 13, and found that they were only marginally undernourished according to the "Harvard" standards for American children of this age group (Jelliffe, 1966). By this time, about four months after the worst of the crisis had passed, it would have been impossible for the casual visitor to find any indication that the Mursi had recently experienced one of the worst periods of food shortage in their history, and worst in living memory.

Comment

This is not the place to draw conclusions about the course which should be taken by future development in the lower Omo valley. But since my account raises a dilemma which has long been familiar to those concerned with economic development in semi-arid areas occupied by pastoralists, I would like to end with a comment on this subject. It appears to be increasingly realized that the modes of subsistence and social organizations of nomadic and transhumant pastoralists represent rational adaptations to marginal environments, and not a sort of primitive half-way house between hunting and settled agriculture (Allen, 1965, p. 287; Grove, 1974, p. 151; Johnson, 1973, pp. 3–4). The dilemma I have just mentioned usually arises after this rational adaptation has been upset by the forces of economic development—after, that is, overstocking and overpopulation have led to the destruction of the environment and to the drastic restoring of ecological balance through "drought". Since the Mursi have not yet experienced, even indirectly, the effects of economic development, it would be possible, in their case, and in the words of the East African Royal Commission, "to let nature to take its course" (quoted by Baker, 1974, p. 176). Such a solution, however, is both practically impossible and morally indefensible, and it is therefore necessary (although it cannot be attempted here) to establish guidelines for development, with the object of keeping social disruption and future hardship to a minimum. An important guideline, for example, would be to utilize the existing skills and interests of the population by developing stock herding for meat production, which is a more efficient means of producing food in a semi-arid environment than dairying (Brown, 1973, pp. 70–71).

But if it is the commitment to economic, technological and scientific growth which, emanating from the West and being taken over by the "developing" nations, has been responsible, in such semi-arid areas, for the drastic restoring of ecological balance through "drought", then it is unlikely that the *ultimate* solution to the problem will lie in the application of yet more western technology. On the contrary, it is likely that the ultimate answer will lie in limits being set to this process of growth in the West. There is something ironic about a situation in which the "experts" deplore the environmental destruction wrought by pastoralists and call for the imposition of maximum limits on animal and human populations when they themselves enjoy a standard of life which has been made possible by a materialist ethic of uninhibited maximization, and which can only be maintained at the cost of massive industrial pollution. From the point of view of the western observer, then, conservation and the limiting of growth should begin at home, for the sake both of his own society and of those which, like that of the Mursi, have yet to suffer the benefits of economic development.

References

ALLAN, W. (1965) *The African Husbandman*. Oliver & Boyd.
BAKER, S. J. K. (1974) "A background to the study of drought in East Africa". In *African Affairs*, **73**, No. 291, pp. 170–171.
BROWN, L. H. (1973) *Conservation for Survival: Ethiopia's Choice*. Haile Sellassie I University.
BUTZER, K. W. (1971) *Recent History of an Ethiopian Delta*. University of Chicago, Department of Geography, Research Paper No. 136.
EVANS-PRITCHARD, E. E. (1951) *Kinship and Marriage among the Nuer*. Oxford University Press.
FIRTH, R. W. (1959) *Social Change in Tikopia*. Macmillan, New York.
GLICKMAN, M. (1971) "Kinship and Credit among the Nuer". In *Africa*, XLI No. 4.
GROVE, A. T. (1974) "Desertification in the African Environment". In *African Affairs*, **73**, No. 291, April, pp. 137–151.
JELLIFFE, D. B. (1966) "The Assessment of the Nutritional Status of the Community". W.H.O. Monograph Series, No. 53.
JOHNSON, DOUGLAS J. (1973) "The Response of Pastoral Nomads to Drought in the Absence of Outside Intervention". Prepared for the United Nations, Office of the Undersecretary General, Special Sahelian Office, December.
LEVI-STRAUSS, C. (1969) *The Elementary Structures of Kinship*. Eyre & Spottiswoode.
MACKENZIE, P. Z. and SIMPSON, R. M. (1971) *The African Veterinary Handbook*. Pitman Publishing.
MAUSS, M. (1954) *The Gift: Forms and Functions of Exchange in Archaic Societies*. Trans. by Ian Cunnison, Cohen and West.
PRATT, D. J., GREENWAY, P. J., GWYNNE, M. D. (1966) "A Classification of East African Rangelands". In *Journal of Applied Ecology*, **3**, 369–82.
SEAMAN, J., HOLT, J. F. J., RIVERS, J. P. W. 1974) *Harerghe Under Drought: A Survey of the Effects of Drought on Human Nutrition in Harerghe Province*. Ethiopian Government Relief and Rehabilitation Commission, May/June.
SPENCER, P. (1974) "Drought and Commitment to Growth". In *African Affairs*, **73**, No. 293.
TURNBULL, C. M. (1972) *The Mountain People*. Jonathan Cape.
TURTON, D. (1973) *The Social Organization of the Mursi*. Unpublished Ph.D. Thesis, London.

AUTHOR INDEX

Bold numerals indicate a paper in this volume

194   HUMAN ECOLOGY IN THE TROPICS

Hirt, H. A. 62, 77
van Hoeve, K. 150, 163
Hoffman, G. 61, 77
Holt, J. F. J. 192
Hopkins, B. 35, 49, 56
Hopkins, G. M. 169
Hosegood, P. H. 57
Hunter, J. M. 93, 94
Hurault, J. 1fn, 2, 3fn, 12fn, 14fn, 17
Hutton, R. G. 37, 57

Illsley, R. 116, 126
Ingram, D. L. 95–112, 95, 99, 106, 110, 111

Jauregui, J. J. 143
Jelliffe, D. B. 190, 192
Johnson, D. J. 165, 168, 191, 192
Jones, E. W. 45, 47, 56
Jones, G. 86
Jordan, P. 137, 141, 142

Kauffman, M. 156, 163
Keay, R. W. J. 49, 56, 79–86
Kerfoot, O. 31, 33, 56
Kershaw, K. A. 49, 56
Kerslake, D.McE. 97, 99, 101, 109, 111
Kesley, W. 57
Knowles, R. J. 134, 143
Koch, R. 87
Kuno, Y. 97, 111
Kuntz, R. E. 140, 142
Kutuza, S. B. 156, 163

Lambrecht, F. L. 156, 163
Langridge, W. P. 179fn
Last, G. C. 132, 142
Latilo, M. 77
Laudelot, H. 29, 37, 56, 57
Leakey, R. E. F. 130, 143
Leblond. 12fn
Leithead, C. S. 110, 112
Leriche, M. 129, 143
Levi-Strauss, C. 178, 192

Lewis, W. A. 80, 86
Lind, A. R. 110, 112
Lyr, H. 61, 77

McCulloch, J. S. G. 33, 57
Macdonald, G. 94
McGavran, E. G. 87, 94
McGregor, I. A. 113, 114, 116, 117, 121, 125, 126
McKelvie, A. D. 31, 57
Mackenzie, P. Z. 179, 192
Mackichan, I. W. 145, 146, 163
Masefield, G. M. 19–26
Masinde, A. 163
Mauss, M. 177, 192
May, J. M. 94
Mayende, J. S. P. 156, 163
Meggers, B. J. 15, 17
Meiklejohn, J. 53, 57
Meyer, H. 153, 163
Moloo, S. K. 156, 163
Monteith, J. L. 99, 106, 111, 112
Morgan, W. B. 27–57, 47, 57, 73, 77
Morris, K. R. S. 152, 163
Moss, R. P. 27–57, 47, 57, 59–77, 73, 77
Mount, L. E. 95, 99, 106, 110, 111
Mwambu, P. M. 151, 156, 163

.

Nelson, W. E. 118, 126
Newton, B. A. 162, 163
Norris, J. M. 63, 77
Nye, P. H. 29, 32, 33, 35, 37, 53, 57

Omaset, P. A. 163
Onyango, R. J. 150, 156, 163

Pasteur, Louis. 87
Paul, B. D. 94
Pavlovskii, E. N. 153, 163
Pereira, H. C. 32, 33, 35, 57
Pesigan, T. P. 136, 143
Peters, E. L. 165fn
Pratt, D. J. 169, 192
Pratt, M. A. C., 33, 56

SUBJECT INDEX

197

List of Contributors

Dr. WILLIAM L. BARTON
World Health Organization, Geneva, Switzerland.

Dr. AUDREY J. BUTT
Department of Ethnology and Prehistory, University of Oxford

Dr. JOHN FORD
2 Forge Close, Horton-cum-Studley, Oxford.

Dr. JAMES P. GARLICK,
Department of Physical Anthropology, University of Cambridge.

Dr. DOUGLAS L. INGRAM
Institute of Animal Physiology, Babraham, Cambridge.

Dr. RONALD W. J. KEAY
Deputy Executive Secretary, The Royal Society, London.

Mr. GEOFFREY B. MASEFIELD
Department of Agricultural Science, University of Oxford.

Professor W. B. MORGAN
Department of Geography, Kings College, London

Professor ROWLAND P. MOSS
Coordinator of Environmental Studies, University of Birmingham.

Professor ANGUS M. THOMSON
M.R.C. Reproduction and Growth Unit, Princess Mary Maternity Hospital, Newcastle-upon-Tyne.

Dr. DAVID TURTON
Department of Social Anthropology, University of Manchester.

Dr. CHRISTOPHER A. WRIGHT
British Museum (Natural History), London.